THE BIG BOOK OF U.S. PRESIDENTS

Written by Victoria Sherrow
Portraits by Bill Prosser
Illustrated by Julian and Janet Baker, Chris Forsey,
Kevin Maddison, and Ann Savage

TEMPLAR

A Templar Book

This edition produced for Reading's Fun Ltd,
119 South Main Street, PO Box 2370, 307 West Burlington,
Fairfield, Iowa 52556.

This book was designed and produced by
The Templar Company plc, Pippbrook Mill, London Road,
Dorking, Surrey RH4 1JE, Great Britain

Designer Janie Louise Hunt
Project Editor Wendy Madgwick
Copy Editor Betsy Bahr Peterson

ISBN 1–898784–24–8

Printed in Italy by L.E.G.O. S.p.A.

Contents

Introduction 4

The Presidential Role 6
George Washington 8
John Adams 10
Thomas Jefferson 11
James Madison 12
James Monroe 13
John Quincy Adams 14
Andrew Jackson 15
Martin Van Buren 16
William H. Harrison 17
John Tyler 18
James K. Polk 19
Zachary Taylor 20
Millard Fillmore 21
Franklin Pierce 22
James Buchanan........... 23
Abraham Lincoln.......... 24
Andrew Johnson 26
Ulysses S. Grant 27
Rutherford B. Hayes 28
James A. Garfield 29

Chester A. Arthur......... 30
Grover Cleveland.......... 31
Benjamin Harrison 32
William McKinley 33
Theodore Roosevelt 34
William Howard Taft 35
Woodrow Wilson.......... 36
Warren G. Harding 37
Calvin Coolidge............ 38
Herbert Hoover............ 39
Franklin D. Roosevelt.... 40
Harry S. Truman........... 42
Dwight D. Eisenhower... 43
John F. Kennedy........... 44
Lyndon B. Johnson 45
Richard M. Nixon 46
Gerald R. Ford 47
Jimmy Carter 48
Ronald Reagan............. 49
George Bush 50
Bill Clinton................... 51

The Presidents and Vice-Presidents 52
Famous Quotes from the Presidents 53
Fun Facts about the Presidents 54
Index 56

Introduction
How Presidents are Elected

Government by the consent of the governed — that has been the guiding principle behind the election of America's leaders since George Washington became the first president. Citizens cast their votes for president in a nationwide election held every four years.

A political party system helps to simplify choices for voters. Today, the main parties are the Democrats and the Republicans. The party system can help voters understand who is running and what they stand for. It can also increase political involvement as people become active in party affairs at the local, state, and national levels.

The election process begins as candidates seek to win their party's nomination for president. Years ago, political party "bosses" often chose presidential candidates. In the early 1900s a new, more democratic system took hold. Primary elections were set up in the states so that people could vote for the candidate they wanted to run.

State party organizations send delegates to a national convention, held during the summer of an election year. There, the delegates officially cast votes for a candidate. During the convention, the party adopts its national platform — the ideas and programs it will present to voters. The business of governing the party for the coming year is also conducted at various meetings. As the nominees for president and vice-president are chosen, the convention-goers celebrate with a great deal of fanfare and speech-making. The national campaign gets underway. Presidential elections can be grueling experiences, as candidates make hundreds of public appearances and take part in televised debates and interviews.

Under the Constitution, the electoral college, rather than the voters themselves, make the final choice of president. Each state has a certain number of electors, the same as the combined number of U.S. senators and representatives. The District of Columbia has three electors. The total for all 50 states is 538, and a candidate must win at least 270 in order to be elected. The parties choose a slate of electors who support the candidate they have nominated. When the people vote, the party of the candidate who has won the most votes is the party whose electors get to cast their vote.

▶ **The Capitol:** *The Capitol in Washington, D.C., is the meeting place of the U.S. Congress. At Lincoln's insistence work on the dome was continued throughout the Civil War as a symbol of national unity. It has changed little since its completion, except for modernizing features such as electricity and central heating.*

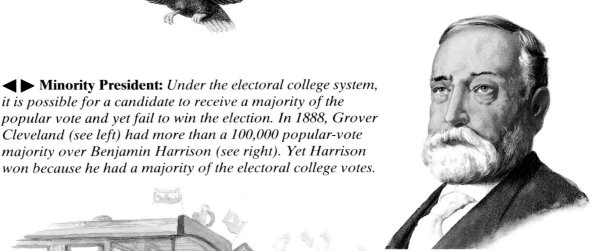

Minority President: *Under the electoral college system, it is possible for a candidate to receive a majority of the popular vote and yet fail to win the election. In 1888, Grover Cleveland (see left) had more than a 100,000 popular-vote majority over Benjamin Harrison (see right). Yet Harrison won because he had a majority of the electoral college votes.*

Campaign Trail: *The media has become a costly and influential tool in a presidential candidate's campaign. In 1860, the Lincoln campaign cost $100,000; by 1960, that amount bought just one half-hour of television air-time.*

Election by the People: *Every four years, each citizen of the United States has the right and duty to vote for a president.*

The Senate: *The vice-president serves as president of the Senate. Senators must be at least 30 years old, U.S. citizens for at least nine years, and residents of the state in which they are elected. Senators are elected for six-year terms, and every two years, one-third of them are either re-elected or replaced. For that reason, the Senate has been called "the house that never dies."*

Victory Celebrations: *To celebrate the new president's inauguration, or arrival in office, the nation's capital hosts speeches, balls, and parades.*

This system gives more populated states greater power. A candidate can become president by winning a smaller number of larger states, rather than a candidate who wins a larger number of smaller ones.

People have criticized the electoral system, because it is possible for candidates to win the presidency in the electoral college even if they have fewer popular votes. This happened in 1824, when John Quincy Adams won the most electoral votes but not the popular vote. In that case, the House of Representatives had the duty of deciding the outcome. This situation also occurred in 1876 (Rutherford B. Hayes) and in 1888 (Benjamin Harrison). "One person, one vote," say advocates of election by direct, popular vote. Supporters of this system maintain that it ensures that the final choice is the person preferred by the country as a whole. However, the U.S. Constitution spells out the system for electing presidents, so an amendment would be necessary to change that system.

The Presidential Role

The Constitution spells out a division of powers among the three branches of government: the executive branch, including the president; the legislative branch, including the Senate and House of Representatives; and the judicial branch, including the Supreme Court and federal courts of appeals. This separation of powers is meant to provide a system of "checks and balances" in the government. No branch has too much or too little power. The powers of the government itself are limited to prevent it from becoming a dictatorship, in which one person, or a small group, rule by force and military might. The government is allowed to do certain things, but only those things.

The president, as head of the executive branch of government, is in charge of enforcing the laws and directing the departments and agencies of the government. The legislative branch, or Congress, makes the laws. The judicial branch interprets the laws and the Constitution, as the supreme law of the land. It settles disputes over these matters.

The president-elect takes office after reciting this traditional oath:

I do solemnly swear (or affirm) that I will faithfully execute the office of President of the United States, and will, to the best of my ability, preserve, protect, and defend the Constitution of the United States.

One of the president's first and most important duties is selecting the people who will serve on the cabinet. George Washington started this custom by naming a group of advisors with whom he could discuss problems and solutions. Other presidents followed the custom. As the government grew in size and complexity, the cabinet members took charge of different executive departments, including labor, the treasury, interior, agriculture, education, state, justice, and defense. As commander-in-chief of the armed forces, the president can ask Congress for a declaration of war.

Each branch of government has ways to "check" the others. While Congress can make a law, the Supreme Court has the power to declare

▼ **Power of the President:** *On President Harry Truman's desk at the White House a small sign read, "The buck stops here." The president has the final say on a large number of problems and decisions.*

THE BUCK STOPS HERE!

◄ **The President's Home:** *The White House has become the symbol of the American presidents. This fine three-storied building with 100 rooms has been home to the U.S. presidents since 1800. Over the years it has undergone many changes.*

such a law unconstitutional. The president may veto a bill passed by Congress, but Congress can override a veto if enough legislators agree to do so. The president can negotiate a treaty, but Congress must then ratify, or approve, it. The president appoints the justices who serve on the Supreme Court, but these appointees must then be approved by Congress. The Supreme Court, in turn, may be called upon to decide whether or not a president has acted in an unconstitutional way. The Senate has the right to impeach the president — that is to accuse him of a high crime — and remove him from office. This sharing of power "balances" the government.

Each year, the president must deliver a State of the Union address, reporting to the Congress on the condition of the country. The president has a duty to propose to Congress necessary measures for the well-being of the nation. The job of president is a challenge. In some cases, it proves an exhausting and frustrating burden to those who have confronted it. Upon leaving office, Rutherford B. Hayes said, "I am heartily tired of this life of bondage, responsibility, and toil." Theodore Roosevelt, on the other hand, said, "No president has ever enjoyed himself as much as I have."

◀ **Chief of State:** *Representing "all Americans," the president is in a unique position to shape public thinking, through press conferences, and radio and television appearances. President Franklin D. Roosevelt conducted his "fireside chats," which were broadcast over the radio, to help gain public support for his programs.*

▶ **Chief Diplomat:** *The Constitution gives the president the responsibility of receiving foreign ambassadors and recognizing foreign governments, such as China and Russia. The conduct of such foreign relations has become an increasingly vital part of the president's job.*

▼ **Commander-in-Chief:** *The Constitution states, "the President shall be commander-in-chief of the Army and Navy of the United States…" A group called the Joint Chiefs of Staff advise the president on military matters, and the president appoints the chairman of the group. In 1951, President Truman (below left) used his power as commander-in-chief to dismiss General Douglas MacArthur (below right), after they disagreed about how to conduct the Korean War. MacArthur had been a popular military hero during World War II and many Americans criticized Truman for this action.*

▲ **The Chief Executive:** *After the President approves a treaty (agreement between two or more countries), at least two-thirds of the members of the Senate must approve it before it becomes law. In an effort to stop the growth of nuclear weapons, President Jimmy Carter concluded the SALT II — Strategic Arms Limitations Talks — Treaty with the Soviet Union.*

George Washington
Federalist 1789–1797

VICE-PRESIDENT: JOHN ADAMS

George Washington has been called "first in war, first in peace, and first in the hearts of his countrymen." His courage, wisdom, and leadership united a new nation and brought him the affectionate title, "father of his country."

Washington was born in 1732 in Westmoreland County, Virginia. During his early years he lived on a plantation. Like other children, he rode horses, went fishing and swimming, and helped with the chores. During his six years of schooling, Washington disliked Latin but loved mathematics. He enjoyed reading about history, geography, farming, and the military and kept notebooks on these subjects.

When Washington was 11, his father died and he went to *Mount Vernon* to live with his older half-brother, Lawrence. As a boy, Washington had wanted to become a sailor, but his mother had disapproved. Instead, his skill with numbers led him to learn surveying — the process of measuring land. At that time, surveyors helped to map frontier lands for new settlements. At the age of 17, Washington began traveling across rivers, mountains, and Indian trails to remote parts of Virginia. He learned to survive in the wilderness.

When Washington was 20, his brother Lawrence died and Washington became the owner of *Mount Vernon*. He began his military career in late 1752 as an adjutant for the Virginia Militia. Afterward, he became a British officer in the French-Indian Wars. In 1775, he was almost

killed while serving as an aide to General Edward Braddock. Three years later, Washington was elected to the Virginia House of Burgesses. He then served as justice of the peace for Fairfax County. He resigned from the military with the rank of colonel. Soon thereafter, in 1759, he married Martha Custis.

During the 1760s, tobacco prices soared and Washington became a wealthy planter. He was highly respected for his military and political activities and was elected to the First and Second Continental Congresses, in 1774 and 1775. Like many others, he had begun to oppose British rule over the colonies.

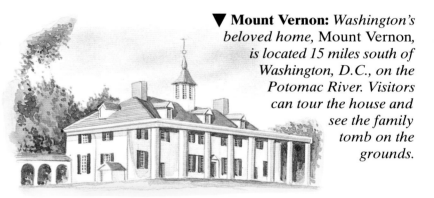

▼ **Mount Vernon:** *Washington's beloved home,* Mount Vernon, *is located 15 miles south of Washington, D.C., on the Potomac River. Visitors can tour the house and see the family tomb on the grounds.*

▲ **Valley Forge:** *When they were encamped at Valley Forge, Pennsylvania, during the harsh winter of 1777–1778, Washington bolstered the spirits of his men. Hungry and lacking warm clothing and boots, the troops stayed together, preparing for the next great battles of the Revolutionary War.*

▶ **The First Lady:** *Martha Dandridge Custis Washington (1731–1802) called herself an "old-fashioned Virginia housekeeper." Like George, she favored a private life at* Mount Vernon *but vowed "to be cheerful" … in whatever situation I may be."*

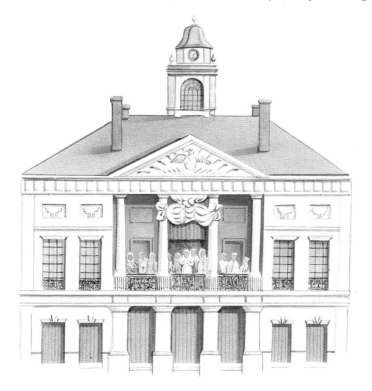

▼ **Federal Hall:** *Washington took the oath of office as president in the Senate Chamber, swearing to "preserve, protect, and defend the Constitution." His public inauguration speech, however, was made from the balcony of Federal Hall in front of cheering crowds.*

◀ **The Bill of Rights:** *Under Washington, the new government developed a firm base, with departments of state, treasury, and war and the U.S. Supreme Court. With his support, Congress approved the Bill of Rights, the first ten amendments to the U.S. Constitution.*

▼ **First U.S. Bank:** *In 1791, Washington signed a bill creating the Bank of the United States. Its main office was opened in Philadelphia on December 12, 1791.*

When war broke out with the British in 1776, Washington was asked to be commander-in-chief of the new Continental Army. At first he protested that he was "not equal to that honor," but he finally accepted the daunting task of organizing the ragged, untrained troops. His strategy of dodging British troops, then attacking from the rear, led one general to call him "a slippery old fox."

After the war ended in 1781, Washington wanted to stay at *Mount Vernon*, but once again he was called to serve. This time he was asked to lead the Constitutional Convention to unite the thirteen states. When the new nation asked him to become its leader, he insisted that he not be called "king." In 1789, he was sworn in as the first U.S.

president. The nation's capital was then in New York, and Washington arrived there on horseback. He wrote to James Madison, "As the first of everything *in our situation* will serve to establish a Precedent. It is devoutly wished on my part, that these precedents may be fixed on true principles."

When his term ended, Washington was persuaded to serve again. As president, Washington urged Americans to stand together — not divide themselves by political parties or regions of the country. He also warned against long-term pacts with foreign nations. He refused to serve a third term and retired to *Mount Vernon*. Washington died of a throat infection just three years later, on December 14, 1799.

John Adams
Federalist 1797–1801

VICE-PRESIDENT: THOMAS JEFFERSON

Devoted to the U.S. Constitution, John Adams once asked, "What other form of government, indeed, can so well deserve our esteem and love?" As president, Adams often expressed his faith in democracy and said that upholding the U.S. Constitution was among his "most serious obligations."

Born on October 30, 1735, in Quincy, Massachusetts, Adams had a privileged childhood. After graduating from Harvard College at the age of 19, he decided to study law. He was admitted to the bar in 1758. Six years later, he married Abigail Smith, the daughter of a clergyman. By then he

▶ **The First Lady:** *Abigail Smith Adams (1744–1818) was deeply concerned about the rights of women. She urged her husband and the other founding fathers to "Remember the ladies!" She and her husband shared intellectual interests as well as deep affection.*

was well known for his political activities. He vigorously opposed the Stamp Act, a tax the British imposed on the colonists in 1765. In 1776, Adams enthusiastically signed the Declaration of Independence. During the Revolutionary War, he served as a diplomat for the colonies in France and Holland, then helped to negotiate peace at the war's end. He was the first U.S. diplomat to England, returning in 1788 to serve as Washington's vice-president.

Adams had expected to succeed Washington as president. But he only narrowly defeated his political foe, Thomas Jefferson, who became vice-president. During a difficult term in office, Adams signed an unpopular treaty with France. The Federalist party also angered many citizens by passing the Alien and Sedition Acts. These acts made criticism of the American government a crime.

In 1800, Adams lost his bid for re-election. He returned home to Massachusetts. In 1825, the Adamses had the pleasure of seeing their son, John Quincy, become the nation's sixth president. One year later, John Adams died at age 90.

▶ **A New Navy:** *In 1797, Adams established a United States Navy. The first ship in the fleet was the 44-gun* United States. *This was followed by the 36-gun* Constellation *and the frigate* Constitution *(see right), later nicknamed "Old Ironsides."*

▲ **The White House:** *In November 1800, the Adamses became the first presidential family to live in the muddy, new capital of Washington, D.C. The White House was only partly finished at the time.*

Thomas Jefferson
Democratic–Republican 1801–1809

VICE-PRESIDENTS: AARON BURR; GEORGE CLINTON

Thomas Jefferson was one of the most talented presidents in history. For this and other reasons, the chief author of the Declaration of Independence was called the "Sage of Monticello."

Jefferson was born in 1743 in Albermarle County, Virginia. A superb student, Jefferson attended William and Mary College in Virginia. After graduating he studied law, entering the bar in 1767. In 1769, he entered the lower house of the colonial legislature, and so began his long career in politics. Jefferson suggested the idea of the First Continental Congress and championed American independence. Years of political thinking emerged as he penned the words, "We hold these truths to be self-evident, that all men are created equal" — words that would begin the Declaration of Independence. In 1779, he became governor of Virginia. Jefferson returned to Congress in 1781. He urged passage of the Bill of Rights, or the first ten amendments to the Constitution. These were meant to ensure that basic rights could never be denied any American. In 1784, he joined Benjamin Franklin as a diplomat in France. Five years later, he became secretary of state in Washington's cabinet.

Jefferson and his supporters opposed the Federalist idea that the wealthy should rule. They formed the Democratic–Republican party. At the next election, in 1800, Jefferson defeated Adams and was elected the nation's third president. He was the first to take office in Washington, D.C., the new capital. After two successful terms, Jefferson chose not to run again. In his later years, he founded the University of Virginia. Jefferson died on July 4, 1826, fifty years after the Declaration of Independence was adopted.

▼ **The First Lady:** *Martha Wayles Skelton Jefferson (1748–1782) was known for her musical talent and intelligence. Jefferson cared for her during her illnesses and grieved deeply when she died.*

◄ **The Louisiana Purchase:** *Jefferson made an advantageous bargain with France to buy the rich territory called the Louisiana Purchase. This allowed the United States to almost double in size, expanding from the Mississippi River to the Rocky Mountains.*

▼ **Great Accomplishments:** *This epitaph, which Jefferson wrote, was inscribed on his tombstone. "Here was buried Thomas Jefferson, author of the Declaration of American Independence, of the Statute of Virginia for Religious Freedom, and Father of the University of Virginia."*

Louisiana Purchase

U.S. (1803)

▼ **Monticello:** *Jefferson designed his beloved red-brick home, Monticello. On the grounds, he enjoyed raising different crops and kept records of his agricultural ventures.*

James Madison
Democratic–Republican 1809–1817

VICE-PRESIDENTS: GEORGE CLINTON; ELBRIDGE GERRY

Weak and sickly as a child, the man James Madison was short and slight. Yet as a statesman and as the "master builder of the Constitution," he towered over others. Chief author of the Bill of Rights, Madison also played a large role in designing the system of checks and balances in the U.S. government. He created the idea of a presidential veto and a judicial branch that could override state laws.

Madison was born at Port Conway, Virginia, on March 16, 1751. His chief interest was his studies. He graduated from Princeton University when just 20 years old. Too frail for military service, Madison entered politics. He was elected to the Virginia assembly in 1776 and worked on the state constitution. After the Revolutionary War, Madison was a key worker on the Constitution

and Bill of Rights. He married Dolley Payne Todd, a widow with one son, in 1794. In 1801, Madison became secretary of state. After Jefferson's second term ended, Madison was elected president. He continued the policies his predecessor had endorsed. Madison reluctantly entered the War of 1812 after the British navy began harassing U.S. ships, seizing cargoes and kidnapping American sailors. The war continued as he began his second term in 1813. After Andrew Jackson achieved an American victory at the Battle of New Orleans in 1815, the war came to an end.

When Madison retired from office two years later, he returned to his Virginia estate, Montpelier. In 1826, he became head of the University of Virginia. Whenever people praised him for the Constitution, he repeatedly said that it was "the work of many heads and many hearts." Madison died at his home at age 85.

▼ **The First Lady:** *Dolley Payne Todd Madison (1768–1849) was charming and gracious. She was a great social asset to her solemn husband, of whom she said, "our hearts understand each other." She was known for her social skills and keen political mind.*

▼ **Religious Freedom:** *Madison ardently supported separation of church and state. Although a member of the Protestant majority (Episcopalian), he insisted that all Americans were "equally entitled to the full and free exercise of their religion."*

▼ **Under Attack:** *When the British burned the Capitol and White House, the president and his wife fled. Dolley, however, managed to save the Declaration of Independence and a portrait of George Washington during their escape.*

James Monroe

Democratic–Republican 1817–1825

VICE-PRESIDENT: DANIEL D. TOMPKINS

The nation's fifth chief executive was known for his tall, neat appearance, quiet dignity, and trustworthiness. Jefferson once said of him, "Monroe is so honest that if you turned his soul inside out there would not be a spot on it."

James Monroe was born in 1758 in Westmoreland County, Virginia. He enrolled in William and Mary College, but left after 2 years to fight for the Continental Army in the Revolutionary War. He became active in politics, supporting Jefferson and the new Democratic-Republican party. In 1786, he married Elizabeth Kortwright, daughter of a Virginian aristocrat. From 1794 to 1796, Monroe served as minister to France. He helped to negotiate the Louisiana Purchase of lands between the Mississippi River and Rocky Mountains. Monroe was highly respected and won his presidential election in 1816 with ease. His re-election in 1820 was unopposed.

His presidency became known as the "Era of Good Feeling." Defeat of the British navy in the War of 1812 had brought fame and honor to the American navy. Other countries began to see the nation as a world power. Monroe valued good relationships among his political leaders, so he chose capable men from different regions to serve in his cabinet. In 1823, Monroe declared that European nations must not claim territory or interfere with countries in the Western Hemisphere. This policy was later called the Monroe Doctrine.

When his second term ended, Monroe retired to his Virginia estate, *Oak Hill*. He became regent at the University of Virginia and presided at the Virginia Constitutional Convention of 1829. Two years later, he died at his daughter's home in New York City.

▶ **The First Lady:** *Elizabeth Kortwright Monroe (1768–1830) was called "la belle Americaine" (the beautiful American) when she lived in France with her husband. At the White House, Elizabeth was known for her formal style of entertaining and elegant clothing.*

▲ **The Missouri Compromise:** *A crisis over slavery occurred in 1820. Missouri wanted to join the Union as a "slave state," but Congress was arguing bitterly over whether slavery should be allowed at all in America. An agreement, called the Missouri Compromise, let Missouri keep slavery but banned it in the northern Louisiana Territory.*

▼ **Five New States:** *America added five new states under Monroe: Maine (1), Mississippi (2), Alabama (3), Illinois (4), and Missouri (5). The population reached 8 million. More land was acquired in a treaty signed with Spain in 1819 when the U.S. took over Florida (6).*

John Quincy Adams
Democratic–Republican 1825–1829

VICE-PRESIDENT: JOHN C. CALHOUN

The son of a former president, John Quincy Adams scorned partisan politics and deal-making. He preferred to act according to his ethics and principles. An accomplished orator, writer, and linguist, he gained the nickname "Old Man Eloquent."

John Quincy Adams was born in 1767 in Braintree (now Quincy), Massachusetts. When he was 10, he sailed for Europe where he attended schools in France and the Netherlands. Adams was so capable that he became private secretary to America's first ambassador to Russia when he was just fourteen.

Adams graduated in law from Harvard College in 1787. When Adams was only 26, George Washington appointed him as minister to the Netherlands. Later, when his father became president, Adams became minister to Prussia. In 1801, he was elected to the Massachusetts senate and two years later became U.S. Senator. In 1809, President Madison sent him as minister to Russia, then to England. On his return in 1817, he became secretary of state under President Monroe.

After a close-run campaign, Adams became president in 1825. As no one had a majority, the election was decided by Congress. During his tenure, Adams proposed several creative new federal projects, including the construction of highways and public buildings. However, opposition from the supporters of Andrew Jackson, whom he had defeated, blocked his ideas.

After a bitter campaign by Jackson's supporters, Adams was badly defeated in the 1828 election and retired to Braintree. In 1830, he agreed to run for Congress and won easily. Adams spoke out forcefully against slavery and for the cause of civil liberties. He collapsed of a stroke in the House of Representatives in 1848 and died two days later.

◀ **The First Lady:** *Louisa Catherine Johnson Adams (1775–1852) was the daughter of an American and his English-born wife. She was the only foreign-born First Lady. Her urbane London background made her more comfortable in Washington than on the family's Massachusetts farm.*

▶ **The "Gag Rule":** *While in Congress, Adams fought the "gag rule," a ban on the reading of antislavery petitions, started by Southern congressmen. These rules were finally abolished so that slavery could be debated along with other issues.*

▼ **The Smithsonian Institution:** *Throughout his life, Adams supported the improvement of the arts and sciences. He ensured that the bequest of Englishman James Smithson would be used to create and endow the Smithsonian Institution as a center of learning.*

Andrew Jackson
Democrat 1829–1837

VICE-PRESIDENTS: JOHN C. CALHOUN; MARTIN VAN BUREN

Jackson got his nickname, "Old Hickory," after a soldier who served with him during the War of 1812 said he was "tough as a hickory." Jackson was the first southern-born president. He was the first president to be elected as a result of popular vote and the first "common man" to reach the nation's highest office.

Andrew Jackson was born near present-day Waxhaw, South Carolina, in 1767. At the age of 13, he joined the army to fight in the Revolutionary War. Despite a limited formal education, he studied law and became a highly respected lawyer. Jackson married Mrs. Rachel Robards, the daughter of Colonel John Donelson. In 1796, Jackson was elected to Congress to represent the new state of Tennessee. During the War of 1812, he led troops to victory against the British in Florida and New Orleans. He ran for the 1824 presidential election, but when none of the four candidates had a majority, Congress broke the stalemate by electing John Quincy Adams.

Jackson won the election of 1828. While president, he supported a strong central government. He ended presidential support for the Bank of the United States, which he said enriched the wealthy at the expense of the common man. After his re-election in 1832, he urged more westward expansion. During this time a number of Native American tribes were removed to limited reservation lands in Indian territory, now Oklahoma. The eastern Cherokee, who had helped him win the Creek War, viewed his actions as a betrayal.

Although in poor health after he left office, Jackson stayed active in managing *The Hermitage*, his Tennessee plantation.
He died in 1845.

◀ **The First Lady:** *Rachel Donelson Jackson (1767–1828) was praised for her gentle, kind nature. She died just a few months before her husband was inaugurated president.*

▼ **The Western Frontier:**
More and more people were "going West" to the new frontiers. In 1830, the first wagon train of settlers crossed the Rocky Mountains to the prairies beyond.

▲ **Battle of the Alamo:** *In 1836, fewer than 200 Texans defended the Alamo mission against a 4,000-strong Mexican army led by General Santa Anna. Although all the Texans were killed, including Jim Bowie and Davy Crockett, the Alamo became a symbol of liberty and independence.*

Martin Van Buren

Democrat 1837–1841

VICE PRESIDENT: RICHARD JOHNSON

Martin Van Buren was a strong leader, nicknamed the "Little Magician" for his shrewd political maneuvers. Van Buren was a loyal follower of Andrew Jackson and supported his policies.

Martin Van Buren was born on December 5, 1782, in Kinderhook, New York. An excellent education enabled him to finish his studies and begin a legal career at age 20. From 1812 to 1820, Van Buren served in the New York senate. For part of that time he was also the state's attorney general.

◀ **The First Lady:** *Hannah Hose Van Buren (1783–1819) had been Van Buren's childhood sweetheart. They married in 1807 after Martin had built up his law practice. Sadly, "Jannette," as her husband called her, using the Dutch name, died of tuberculosis before her husband was elected president.*

▶ **Financial Panic:** *Van Buren's early presidency was marked by financial panic and economic disaster. Banks failed, unemployment rose, cotton prices fell, and there was a shortage of flour due to crop failure. This led to great national unrest. In New York, the high cost of flour even led to riots.*

◀ **Aroostook War:** *Van Buren ended the armed clashes over the U.S. northeast boundary with Canada. Both the U.S. and Canada claimed the Aroostook Valley. Talks were set up which eventually led to the Webster–Ashburton Treaty of 1842.*

He took charge of the state's Democratic–Republican party and shaped its major policies. When he joined the U.S. Senate in 1821, Van Buren supported Andrew Jackson. Van Buren was also a major force in organizing the new Democratic party when the main party split.

During Jackson's first term, Van Buren served as secretary of state. During Jackson's second term, he was vice-president. Van Buren won the 1836 presidential election by a wide margin. Soon after he entered office, financial panic swept the country.

Hundreds of U.S. banks failed, while many others closed. Many people blamed Jackson's monetary policies for this disaster. In addition, the arguments over slavery were deepening, and legislators were disagreeing bitterly over the annexation of Texas. Van Buren lost his bid for re-election in 1840.

Back in New York, the former president remained active in local and national politics, speaking out against slavery. He died at home in Kinderhook at the age of 79.

William H. Harrison

Whig March–April 1841

VICE-PRESIDENT: JOHN TYLER

William Henry Harrison was a wealthy man, the son of a well-known politician. Yet he was best known as a soldier. Harrison's presidential campaign was carefully planned. His party managers groomed his image as a "man of the people" to appeal to the general voter.

Harrison was born in 1773 to a wealthy family in Berkeley Plantation, Virginia. His father had been governor of Virginia. Harrison joined the army in 1791, rising to the rank of captain. In 1798, he left the army to become secretary to the Northwest Territory. Two years later, he was appointed governor of the Indiana Territory. He became a military hero when he suppressed an uprising by Native Americans at the Battle of Tippecanoe. In the War of 1812, he defeated the British at the Battle of Thames near what is now Ontario, Canada. Later, Harrison was elected to the Ohio senate and the U.S. House of Representatives.

In 1840, the Whigs chose Harrison as their presidential nominee. They thought that Harrison's military feats would help him win. During the campaign he became known as "Old Tippecanoe." After John Tyler was chosen as vice-president, one of the campaign slogans became "Tippecanoe and Tyler too." The Whigs criticized their opponent, Martin Van Buren, for his aristocratic tastes and manners.

Harrison was elected by a large majority and took the oath of office in March, 1841. Unfortunately, he succumbed to pneumonia on April 4th and became the first president to die in office.

▼ **The Battle of Tippecanoe:** *Harrison made his name at the Battle of Tippecanoe in 1811, when his army defeated the Shawnee Indians at Prophetstown.*

▲ **The First Lady:** *Anna Tuthill Symmes Harrison (1775–1864) was the daughter of a wealthy landowner, Judge John Cleve Symmes. She married Harrison, then an army lieutenant, in 1796.*

◄ **Log Cabins and Cider:** *The Whigs got the idea for their 1840 "log cabin and cider" campaign to emphasize Harrison's frontier image from the Democrats. A Democratic newspaper had chided Harrison by saying, "Give him a barrel of hard cider and … he will sit by the fire and study moral philosophy."*

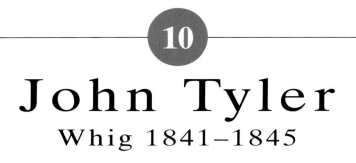

John Tyler
Whig 1841–1845

VICE-PRESIDENT: NONE

John Tyler was the first man to become president after a chief executive died. He faced strong opposition. Enemies called him "Acting President" and "His Accidency." However, he stuck to his beliefs and rejected ideas he thought wrong for the nation.

John Tyler was born in 1790 at *Greenways Estate*, his father's plantation, in Charles City County, Virginia. He studied law at William and Mary College. At 21, Tyler was elected to the Virginia legislature. After five years in state government, he was sent to the U.S. House of Representatives. During those years, Tyler was a Democrat, but his party criticized him for disagreeing with some of their policies. They called him "Turncoat Tyler," prompting him to switch to the Whig party. As before, his independence led to conflicts with his new party. Yet in 1840, party leaders asked him to run for vice-president. They hoped he would attract Southern voters and people who supported states' rights.

As president, Tyler again showed his independence. The Whig party announced that he was no longer a member of their party. The entire cabinet resigned except for Secretary of State Daniel Webster. Despite this, Tyler's administration achieved a great deal. It reorganized the U.S. Navy and founded the U.S. Weather Bureau. In 1842, Tyler ended the Second Seminole War and signed the Webster-Ashburton Treaty, which ended a Canadian border dispute.

With no party to support him, Tyler was defeated in the 1844 election. He retired to Virginia but later returned to public life in 1861, when he worked to find a compromise to avoid the Civil War. Later he joined the Confederate government, serving in its House of Representatives until his death in 1862.

Letitia Tyler

▶ **The First Ladies:** *Letitia Christian Tyler (1790–1842) was called "the most entirely unselfish person you can imagine" by her daughter-in-law, Priscilla Cooper Tyler. An invalid when Tyler became president, she was the first president's wife to die in the White House.*

In 1844, Tyler remarried. Julia Gardiner (1820–1889), a vivacious, sociable New Yorker, was First Lady during the last eight months of Tyler's presidency.

Julia Gardner

◀ **The State of Texas:** *Texas had become an independent republic in 1836, with Sam Houston as its governor. Tyler championed the annexation of Texas and in 1845, just before he left office, Texas became part of the Union.*

Texas 1836

Texas 1845

James K. Polk

Democrat 1845–1849

VICE-PRESIDENT: GEORGE M. DALLAS

James K. Polk was a self-proclaimed fighter for the common people. He once declared he would work hard to keep politicians from shifting money "from the pockets of the people to the favored classes." A supporter of Andrew Jackson, he was the last of the Jacksonians to serve as president.

James Polk was born in 1795 in Mecklenburg County, North Carolina. When he was 11 the family moved to Tennessee, where he helped his father, a surveyor, on the family farm. Polk graduated from the University of North Carolina, where he studied law, in 1818. A successful lawyer, he won a seat in the Tennessee house of representatives. In 1825, Polk became the youngest member of the U.S. House of Representatives. He supported his party leaders' policies, and his loyalty, speaking skills, and hard work led to his selection as Speaker of the House

from 1835 to 1839. He then left Congress to become governor of Tennessee, but he was not re-elected in 1842.

In 1844, Polk became the Democratic party's surprise choice for president, mainly because of his clear support for the annexation of Texas. During his second year in office, in a boundary dispute, Mexican troops fired on U.S. soldiers. Polk urged Congress to declare war. The U.S. won the war within a year, and Mexico gave up land that later became the states of California, Nevada, Utah, Arizona, and New Mexico.

Polk achieved other goals, including lowering tariffs and acquiring the Oregon territory. He also set up a separate U.S. treasury. After serving only one term, he retired to his home in Nashville in May 1849. A few months later he died of cholera.

▼ **The Dark Horse:** *Polk was the nation's first "dark horse" candidate — an unexpected choice who was not given much chance to win. Despite this, he had a successful tenure and achieved many of his goals, including acquiring most of the Oregon territory from Great Britain.*

▲ **The First Lady:** *Sarah Childress Polk (1803–1891) was serene and well-educated. She often helped her husband with his speeches and other political work.*

▶ **The Mexican War:** *Polk strongly believed in "Manifest Destiny" — that the U.S. should expand across North America. The capture of Mexico City by U.S. troops and the winning of the Mexican War brought vast land gains.*

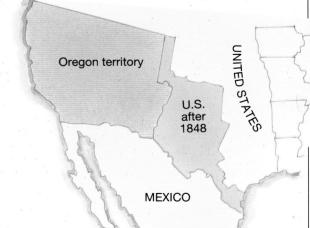

Oregon territory

U.S. after 1848

UNITED STATES

MEXICO

Zachary Taylor
Whig 1849–1850

VICE-PRESIDENT: MILLARD FILLMORE

Named "Old Rough and Ready" for his military feats, Zachary Taylor considered himself unqualified for the presidency. An honest, hard-working man, he tried to fulfill his task by appointing able people to cabinet posts.

Zachary Taylor was born in 1784 in Orange County, Virginia. Soon after, the family moved to a Kentucky plantation. Taylor decided to follow in his father's footsteps and become a soldier. He pursued a military career rather than formal education, and by 1808 he had become a first lieutenant. Two years later, he was promoted to captain. His bravery during the War of 1812 led to his being made a major. In 1846, when the U.S. declared war on Mexico, Taylor commanded 4,000 soldiers sent to defend the Rio Grande. Under his leadership, the U.S. Army won the war and Taylor was hailed as a national hero.

The Whig party asked him to run for president in 1848, hoping that his fame would enable them to recapture the White House. After Taylor won, he surprised party leaders by showing his independence and desire to lead by his own principles. The great issue of his presidency was the status of the newly acquired Mexican territories. Taylor wanted to admit California and New Mexico to the Union, but Southerners opposed this as it would re-open the slavery debate. The Senate favored a compromise, but Taylor would not give in. Then, after only 16 months in office, Taylor died following a brief illness in July 1850.

◀ **The First Lady:** *Margaret Mackall Smith Taylor (1788–1852), the daughter of a Maryland planter, married Taylor in 1810. She lived alongside her soldier husband on the frontier. She disliked White House social events, so one of her five daughters, Betty Taylor Bliss, served as official hostess.*

▶ **The Gold Rush:** *With the California gold rush of 1849 and many new inventions and industries, America was prosperous during Taylor's short administration.*

◀ **The Military Hero:** *Taylor made his reputation during the Mexican War. His victory over the Mexican General Santa Anna at Buena Vista gave the United States control of northern Mexico.*

Millard Fillmore

Whig 1850–1853

Millard Fillmore's rise to the presidency showed again that humble birth need not prevent a person from reaching the nation's highest office. Fillmore was praised for his honest character even by people who disagreed strongly with his policies.

Fillmore was born in 1800 at Locke in western New York state. At 14, he became a wool carder's apprentice. Five years later, he bought his release from his apprenticeship. Between 1819 and 1823, Fillmore studied law. He was admitted to the bar and became a respected attorney in his state.

Fillmore was elected to Congress as a Whig. He became close to such prominent men as Henry Clay, Daniel Webster, and John Calhoun. Fillmore ran for governor of New York state in 1844 but was defeated. He was elected state comptroller in 1847 and, the next year, his party chose him to run as vice-president with war hero Zachary Taylor.

When President Taylor died in 1850, Fillmore became the chief executive. Debates over slavery dominated Fillmore's term. Northern Whigs wanted to ban all slavery in new states and territories, which included California. Fillmore sought to appease both sides of the slavery issue. He urged Congress to pass a series of bills, together known as the Compromise of 1850. They abolished the slave trade in the District of Columbia, admitted California as a free state, and imposed a stricter fugitive slave law. First celebrated as a great success, these measures soon lost favor among Northern opponents of slavery.

Fillmore did not join the new Republican party and he was not nominated for a second term. After losing that election, Fillmore returned to Buffalo, New York. He continued to take an active role in political affairs, though he never again ran for public office. Fillmore died in 1874.

▼ **The Slavery Issue:** *Fillmore's compromising stand on slavery led Harriet Beecher Stowe to publish* Uncle Tom's Cabin *in 1852. Her book dramatized the evils of slavery and strengthened antislavery feelings among Northerners.*

▲ **The First Lady:**
Abigail Powers Fillmore (1798–1853) met her husband at an academy in New Hope, New York, in 1819. As a teacher, she was the first First Lady to work after marriage. An avid reader, she established a library in the White House.

◄ **Countrywide Links:** *In the early 1840s, Fillmore had supported granting money to Samuel Morse to develop his telegraph, another way to link distant parts of the country.*

Franklin Pierce
Democrat 1853–1857

VICE-PRESIDENT: WILLIAM R. KING

A well-to-do New Englander, Franklin Pierce was criticized for his proslavery sentiments. He had spoken hopefully of peace and prosperity during his inaugural address, but he was unable to stem the tide of the slavery conflict.

Franklin Pierce was born in 1804 in Hillsborough, New Hampshire. His father, a Revolutionary War general, later became governor of the state. After graduating from Bowdoin College in Maine, he attended law school in Northampton, Massachusetts. He was admitted to the bar in 1827 and began practicing law in New Hampshire.

Pierce ran for the state legislature as a Democrat in 1829 and served as Speaker of the House from 1831 to 1833. From there he went to the U.S. Congress, followed by five years in the Senate, where he joined those who opposed the abolitionist (antislavery) movement. He also supported the Compromise of 1850 and did not upset Southern voters. These factors led to his selection as a "dark-horse" Democratic candidate for president in 1852.

As president, Pierce was criticized for a lack of leadership. He supported Stephen Douglas's Kansas-Nebraska bill, which allowed settlers in those two western territories to decide for themselves whether or not to allow slavery. This sharpened hostilities between free and slave states. Groups of settlers fought violently for control in those territories. "Bleeding Kansas," as the area was called, represented a major crisis leading to the Civil War.

Pierce did not gain his party's nomination a second time. He died in 1869 at Concord, New Hampshire.

▲ **The First Lady:** *Jane Means Appleton Pierce (1806–1863), a minister's daughter, was frail and sensitive. Mrs. Robert E. Lee wrote of her, "Her health was a bar to any great effort on her part … but she was a refined, extremely religious, and well-educated lady."*

▶ **Japanese Contacts:** *Urged by American whaling and manufacturing interests, President Fillmore had sent Commodore Matthew Perry and navy ships to Japan. In 1854, Pierce received Perry's report that he had been successful and that U.S. ships would have access to Japanese ports.*

▲ **The New Railway:** *Pierce promoted an increase in the size of the United States. He approved spending $10 million on more land in the Southwest, making way for a southerly route for the transcontinental railway, started during Fillmore's presidency.*

James Buchanan

Democrat 1857–1861

VICE-PRESIDENT: JOHN C. BRECKINRIDGE

When James Buchanan took office in 1857, the nation was on the brink of war. He tried to heal the rifts between North and South, in the nation and in Congress, but failed. He was called a "do-nothing" who pleased nobody, by taking a course that aimed to appease both sides.

James Buchanan was born in 1791 near Mercersburg, Pennsylvania. He graduated from Dickinson College in 1809 and then studied law at Lancaster. He enlisted in the army during the War of 1812 but did not enjoy military life. Returning home, he devoted himself to politics. A superb debater, he won five consecutive elections to Congress, beginning in 1821. Buchanan served as minister to Russia and in 1834 won election to the Senate. In 1845, Polk made him secretary of state, then Pierce sent him to England as ambassador in 1853.

Buchanan was abroad during the arguments on slavery and so had escaped public involvement. He was viewed as a "safe" choice for the Democratic nomination in 1856. As president, Buchanan avoided the slavery issue by focusing on Cuba and Central America. He supported the Union but said Southern states should be able to secede (leave the United States). In 1861, Confederate troops fired at *Star of the West*, a troop ship that he had sent to Fort Sumter, South Carolina. War seemed imminent.

Buchanan chose not to run again and retired to Lancaster, Pennsylvania. During the Civil War, he remained loyal to the Union and to President Lincoln. He died at his home in 1868.

▶ **The Official Hostess:** *The first and only bachelor president, Buchanan had planned to marry after the War of 1812, but his fiancée died. His niece, Harriet Lane, who served as official hostess, charmed people with her enthusiasm and the care she took to seat political rivals apart at White House dinner parties.*

▶ **Dred Scott:** *In 1857, the U.S. Supreme Court ruled on the controversial Dred Scott case. Scott, a former slave, had lived for over two years in free territory where he hoped to remain free. The Court ruled that Negros were "property," not citizens, and that the Missouri Compromise was unconstitutional.*

▼ **Pony Express:** *In April 1860, the first Pony Express rider delivered mail to Sacramento, California, after an 11-day non-stop journey from Missouri.*

Dred Scott

John Brown

▶ **John Brown:** *The slavery issue continued to cause violence. White abolitionist John Brown was hanged as a traitor for trying to start a slave rebellion in Harper's Ferry, West Virginia.*

Abraham Lincoln
Republican 1861–1865

VICE-PRESIDENTS: HANNIBAL HAMLIN; ANDREW JOHNSON

mother, Nancy Hanks, died. His father's new wife, Sarah Bush Johnston, encouraged Lincoln to read the books she had brought from Kentucky — the Bible, Weem's biography of George Washington, and Shakespeare's plays. By his teens, Lincoln was tall and lanky, and grew strong clearing timber and splitting logs to make fences. At 19, he traveled up and down the Mississippi on a flatboat delivering farm products. When his family moved to Illinois, he rejoined them and worked as a store clerk, a postmaster, and a surveyor of New Salem.

◀ **The First Lady:** *Mary Todd Lincoln (1818–1882) had a privileged youth, saddened by her mother's death when she was 7. Mary was criticized for her moodiness and extravagance, but her husband, as president, recalled falling in love with her and said, "I have never fallen out."*

▼ **The Illinois Railsplitter:** *As a young man in Illinois, Lincoln put his axeman's skill to use on a contract to split 3,000 fence rails. This led to him being known as "The Railsplitter" in later political life.*

During his 1858 campaign for senator from Illinois, Abraham Lincoln uttered these famous words, "A house divided against itself cannot stand … I believe this government cannot endure permanently half slave and half free." Lincoln lost the election but gained great support in the North, which helped him to win the presidency two years later.

One of America's most honored presidents, Abraham Lincoln was born on February 12, 1809, in a log cabin in Hardin County, Kentucky. When he was 7, the family moved to Indiana, where his

▼ The 13th Amendment: *In 1865, at Lincoln's urging, Congress passed the 13th Amendment to the Constitution, officially abolishing slavery. It read: "Neither slavery nor involuntary servitude, except as a punishment for crime, whereof the party shall have been duly convicted, shall exist within the United States…"*

▲ The Last Battle: *The end of the Civil War came when the Confederate capital, Richmond, fell to the Union army on April 3, 1865. The city was left in ruins.*

▼ Gettysburg Address: *At the dedication of the military cemetery at Gettysburg, Lincoln made one of his most famous speeches. He said, "We here highly resolve that these dead shall not have died in vain — that this nation, under God, shall have a new birth of freedom — and that government of the people, by the people, and for the people, shall not perish from the earth."*

▶ The Lincoln Memorial: *The Lincoln Memorial is one of the most often visited monuments in Washington, D.C. The words under Lincoln's figure read: "In this temple, as in the hearts of the people for whom he saved the Union, the memory of Abraham Lincoln is enshrined forever."*

Lincoln's wide grin and talent for telling stories helped make him popular. In 1834, he ran for the state legislature and went on to serve four terms. He also studied law and formed a successful practice at Springfield, the state capital. Lincoln was against the idea of slavery. In 1858, he and Stephen Douglas took part in seven famous debates on the spread of slavery. Their debates were widely reported and Lincoln became known across America.

In 1860, "Honest Abe" won the battle for president. Southerners formed the Confederate States of America under their leader, Jefferson Davis. However, Lincoln refused to allow the South to leave the Union, and the Civil War began on April 12, 1861. After the bloody Battle of Antietam the next year, Lincoln delivered his famous Emancipation Proclamation in 1863, declaring all slaves free. The war dragged on as Lincoln won re-election in 1864. After four years of fighting, the Southern commander, General Robert E. Lee, surrendered on April 9, 1865. At his second inauguration, Lincoln pledged to "bind up the nation's wounds" and restore peace "with malice toward none; with charity for all."

Before he could fulfill his goal of a compassionate postwar reconstruction, Lincoln was assassinated by actor John Wilkes Booth in Ford's Theatre. He died on April 15, 1865.

Andrew Johnson

Democrat 1865–1869

VICE-PRESIDENT: NONE

Like his predecessor Abraham Lincoln, Andrew Johnson was born poor and had to educate himself. He was the only Southern senator to support the Union and refuse to join the Confederacy. For this stance, he was labeled a traitor by his adopted state of Tennessee.

Andrew Johnson was born in 1808 in Raleigh, North Carolina. By age 14, he was apprenticed to a tailor who treated him poorly. Johnson ran away to live on his own. In his spare time, he taught himself to read and write, studying any books he could borrow. In 1826, he settled in Tennessee, earning a meager living as a tailor. In Greeneville, he married Eliza McCardle, whose good education helped him to improve his own. In 1830, he became mayor of Greenville and then served in the state legislature until 1843.

Elected to the U.S. House of Representatives, then to the Senate, Johnson championed the common people and promoted a homestead bill to give land to poor settlers. As governor of Tennessee in 1853, he fought for state support of public schools.

When Lincoln won a second term in 1864, Johnson was the vice-presidential candidate and represented southerners who supported the Union. When Lincoln was killed only six weeks after his inauguration, Johnson became president. Congress soon tried to pass numerous bills intended to punish the former Confederate states, but Johnson vetoed them, attempting to keep Lincoln's promise of a fair-minded peace.

Johnson returned to Tennessee after his term ended. In 1875, he finally regained his old Senate seat, but he died a few months later at age 66.

► **The First Lady:** *Eliza McCardle Johnson (1810–1876) reared five children, while helping her husband in his career. In poor health after the war, she entrusted her daughter, Martha Patterson, with White House social duties.*

◄ **Trial for Impeachment:** *Johnson was the first president to face possible impeachment when the Senate accused him of not following a law they had passed. But the eventual vote was in Johnson's favor.*

◄ **On the Breadline:** *The South faced economic ruin after the war. Confederate money was worthless, and banks and businesses that had depended on the government went bankrupt. Hungry people waited in breadlines in cities, such as New Orleans.*

► **Tennessee's Military Governor:** *Lincoln appointed Johnson military governor of Tennessee during the Civil War. In this demanding post, Johnson tried to calm rebellious citizens. Eastern Tennessee stayed loyal to the Union and the state sent representatives to the U.S. Congress as of 1864. The State was readmitted to the Union in 1866.*

Ulysses S. Grant
Republican 1869–1877

VICE-PRESIDENTS: SCHUYLER COLFAX; HENRY WILSON

As leader of the Union army, Ulysses S. Grant was a stubborn fighter. Yet at the war's end, he said Americans should seek "peace without victory." As president, Grant faced the enormous challenge of reconstruction.

He was born Hiram Ulysses Grant in 1822 at Point Pleasant, Ohio, and grew up in nearby Georgetown. Grant's father convinced a local congressman to get his son appointed to the army academy at West Point, New York, where he was registered as "Ulysses Simpson Grant." He decided to keep that name. In 1843, Grant fought in the Mexican War, winning two medals for heroism. When the Civil War began, he rejoined the army and organized the Illinois regiment. By 1861, he was made brigadier general of volunteers. He was promoted to major general in 1862. After winning the battles of Vicksburg and Chattanooga in 1863, Lincoln named him commander of all the Union armies. He accepted the surrender of Confederate General Robert E. Lee at Appomatox Court House, Virginia, on April 9, 1865.

A hero in the North, the Republicans nominated him for president in 1868, even though Grant lacked political experience. His first term was marred by political scandal, but he successfully overcame this problem and was re-elected in 1872. Corruption by dishonest advisors had hurt Grant's reputation, but it appears that he himself was honest. America suffered an economic depression in 1873, which further deepened the nation's problems.

After leaving office in 1877, Grant toured the world and wrote his *Memoirs*, which were published after his death in 1885.

▲ **The First Lady:** *Julia Dent Grant (1826–1902) was glad to move into the White House after years of living on various army posts and worrying about her husband's safety. The Grants enjoyed a long, happy marriage.*

▲ **Chicago Fire:** *A disaster during Grant's term was the Chicago fire of 1871. It destroyed more than three square miles of buildings and killed 250 people.*

▶ **A Generous General:** *Upon accepting Lee's offer of surrender in 1865, Grant won hearts by refusing to accept Lee's sword and for letting the Southern soldiers keep their horses "for the spring plowing."*

▶ **The Ku Klux Klan:** *During Grant's presidency, Congress passed two acts to try to protect black voting rights from interference by the Ku Klux Klan.*

Rutherford B. Hayes
Republican 1877–1881

VICE-PRESIDENT: WILLIAM A. WHEELER

Rutherford B. Hayes became president at a time when Americans were losing faith in government after years of political scandals and economic problems. Sincere and hard-working, he restored hope with an honest administration. He worked to make the still war torn nation more secure.

Rutherford B. Hayes was born in 1822 in Delaware, Ohio. An avid reader, he graduated at the top of his class at Kenyon College, then attended Harvard Law School. In 1845, he returned to his home state to practice law. When the Civil War began, Hayes volunteered and helped to organize a military company, which fought in several violent battles. He rose to brevet major general and was cited for bravery. While still at war, he was elected to the Ohio state congress but did not take his seat until peace was declared. In 1867, he was elected governor of Ohio and served three terms.

In 1876, Hayes won the Republican party's nomination for the presidency. The election was so close that an electoral commission met to decide the outcome (185 to 184 electoral votes for Hayes). As president, Hayes was determined to end weak reconstruction policies that had caused problems in the South. He removed federal troops and called for "wise, honest, and local self-government" and outlawed "carpetbagging," in which Northerners went to the South to exploit the financial misfortunes. In 1879, Congress agreed to let people redeem the paper money that had been issued during the Civil War for gold. Hayes also proposed legislation that laid the groundwork for future civil service reforms.

Although he was only 59 in 1881, Hayes chose not to seek a second term. He retired to spend his last years in supporting government reforms, education, and religious charities. Hayes died in 1893 in Fremont, Ohio.

▶ **The First Lady:** *Lucy Ware Webb Hayes (1831–1889), a college graduate and mother of eight, was called "Lemonade Lucy" when she banned alcoholic beverages from the White House. During the Civil War, she nursed soldiers in her husband's regiment.*

▲ **The Commission's Choice:** *As a nominee for president, the little-known Hayes embarked on a busy campaign, with torchlight parades, soapbox speeches, and many public appearances. After a close-run campaign, an electoral commission decided that Hayes, rather than his opponent Samuel Tilden, should be president.*

◀ **On Strike:** *When riots broke out in several states as a result of the railroad strikes of 1877, Hayes sent federal troops to restore order.*

James A. Garfield
Republican March–September 1881

VICE-PRESIDENT: CHESTER A. ARTHUR

In 1865, James Garfield worked to calm an angry mob that had gathered in the wake of President Lincoln's assassination. Some 16 years later, he became the second president to be assassinated in office.

The last president to be born in a log cabin, James Abram Garfield was born in 1831 in Orange, Ohio. When he was only 2 years old, his father died, leaving his mother to raise four children in poverty. Garfield held local farm jobs and drove a team of horses on the Ohio Canal. At age 18, he attended Western Reserve Eclectic Institute (now Hiram College) at Hiram, Ohio. From 1854 to 1856, he completed his degree at Williams College in Massachusetts. He then studied law. At age 26, he became principal of Hiram College. He was elected to the Ohio senate in 1859.

When the Civil War broke out, Garfield joined the Union army. He commanded a volunteer regiment, and was promoted to colonel, then to major general. He resigned in 1863 after being elected to Congress. For seventeen years, Garfield served as a representative and was known as a leader among his fellow Republicans. He was a powerful speaker and preached against slavery.

▶ **The First Lady:** *Lucretia Rudolph Garfield (1832–1918) was a reserved, literary mother of seven. Her husband spoke of her "tact and faultless taste," and the two were close companions.*

▼ **A Welcome Sight:** *When Garfield arrived in Washington for his inauguration, he was pleased to see former ex-Confederate soldiers waving the U.S. flag. Garfield spoke hopefully about bringing the country together, saying, "Our people are determined to leave behind them all those bitter controversies."*

In 1880, Garfield was elected to the U.S. Senate. That same year, he became a reluctant presidential candidate and won, despite opposing factions within his party. Not long afterward, Garfield was shot as he entered a Washington railway station on July 2, 1881. He was on his way to a reunion at Williams College. His assassin, Charles Guiteau, was angry that he had not been named U.S. consul to France. Garfield died from his wounds on September 19th. He was buried in Cleveland, Ohio.

▶ **Light On!** *In October 1879, Thomas A. Edison developed the first commercially successful electric lamp at his laboratory at Menlo Park, New Jersey. Within 2 years the first street lights were being installed.*

Chester A. Arthur
Republican 1881–1885

VICE-PRESIDENT: NONE

When "Chet" Arthur was thrust into office after Garfield's death, many people doubted that he was up to the job. Arthur had long been associated with political bosses who sold favors. However, he became a respected statesman who worked hard for reform.

Chester Alan Arthur was born in 1829 in Fairfield, Vermont. He graduated in 1848 from Union College in Schenectady, New York, and became one of the best known lawyers in New York City. He represented the civil rights of black Americans before the Civil War. In 1859, he married Ellen Herndon and the couple had three children, of whom two survived.

After joining the Republican party, Arthur took part in state and city politics. In 1871, President Grant appointed him collector of customs for the Port of New York. President Hayes later removed him from that office because he gave jobs in the customs department to friends and political supporters. This was a common practice among many office-holders of the day.

In the 1880 presidential campaign, Arthur was elected as vice-president. The man with the thick side whiskers and friendly ways was scarcely known to most Americans when he had to take on the role of president just a few months after Garfield's inauguration. A month before he took office, Arthur's beloved wife Ellen died suddenly.

Fears about Arthur's qualifications waned as he appointed people of high character to office. He championed reforms to ensure that jobs were awarded on the basis of merit, not political patronage. Despite his many successes, Arthur was less popular near the end of his term. He did not press to be nominated for president in 1884. Two years later, Arthur died in New York City.

▶ **The First Lady:** *Ellen Lewis Herndon Arthur (1837–1880), a talented contralto, sang in Washington's St. John's Episcopal Church choir. After she died, Arthur presented a stained glass window to the church in her honor and had it placed where he could see it from his office.*

◀ **The Red Cross:**
The American Red Cross was organized after years of effort by Clara Barton, a battlefield nurse during the Civil War. She later undertook relief work throughout the world.

▲ **Brooklyn Bridge:** *In 1883, the Brooklyn Bridge was completed in New York City. It was one of the most remarkable engineering achievements of the century.*

Grover Cleveland

Democrat 1885–1889; 1893–1897

VICE-PRESIDENTS: THOMAS A. HENDRICKS; ADLAI E. STEVENSON

Grover Cleveland was the only person ever to serve two unsuccessful terms in office. Called "Grover the Good" by admirers, he was a strong leader known for his efforts to improve and reform government. He refused to play politics, saying, "What is the use of being elected or re-elected unless you stand for something?"

Stephen Grover Cleveland was born into an old and respected family in 1837 in Caldwell, New Jersey. After his father's death in 1853, Cleveland studied law and began work in Buffalo, New York, as a clerk in a law office. In 1859, he passed the bar exam. Cleveland was elected mayor of Buffalo in 1881. Later, he became the governor of New York and helped Theodore Roosevelt to reform the New York City government.

In 1884, Cleveland became the first Democratic president elected after the Civil War. He strongly supported civil service reform. Labor disputes and strikes were becoming more common, but Congress did not follow Cleveland's advice to set up a labor arbitration board. The American Federation of Labor, a union organization, was founded in 1886.

A bachelor before his election, Cleveland became the first president to marry in the White House, in 1886. He and 22-year-old Frances Folsom exchanged vows in the Blue Room. His refusal to deal with political bosses led to his defeat for re-election in 1888. Cleveland continued to be active within his party and was nominated for president once again in 1892. He beat Benjamin Harrison, the man who had defeated him four years earlier. Among the problems he faced during his second administration were increasing unemployment, lower wages, and continuing labor troubles.

When Cleveland's second term ended in 1897, he retired to Princeton, New Jersey. He became a trustee of Princeton University as well as a popular lecturer and writer. He died in 1908.

▲ **Great Monuments:** *The Washington Monument, the world's tallest stone monument, was dedicated in 1885. Another monument, the Statue of Liberty, a gift from France, was also dedicated under Cleveland's first administration in 1886.*

▲ **The First Lady:** *Frances Folsom Cleveland (1864–1947), a native of Buffalo, New York, was the youngest of the First Ladies. She gave birth to two of her five children in the White House.*

▲ **New Americans:** *European immigrants flooded into America in the late 19th century. A literacy test for foreigners was debated in Congress in an attempt to limit entry, but President Cleveland vetoed the bill.*

Benjamin Harrison
Republican 1889–1893

VICE-PRESIDENT: LEVI P. MORTON

At 5 feet 6 inches, "Little Ben," as he was called, was the grandson of President William H. Harrison. Because of the electoral college system, he won the election of 1888, although his opponent had more popular votes.

Benjamin Harrison was born in 1833 in North Bend, Ohio. Harrison graduated from Miami University in 1852. After studying law, he built a respected practice in Indianapolis, Indiana. In the Civil War, Harrison served with the Indiana regiment. He won a medal for bravery during the Atlanta campaign, becoming a brigadier general by the war's end.

Harrison ran for state governor of Indiana in 1876, but lost. However, in 1881, Harrison succeeded in his bid for the U.S. Senate. During his term there, he supported civil service reforms and restrictions on Chinese immigration. This led to the Chinese Exclusion Act of 1892, which was passed when he was president. He also fought for the concerns of homesteaders, Native Americans, and veterans.

The presidential election of 1888 was dominated by the conflict over tariffs. Cleveland wanted to lower the high protective tariff on imported goods, but Harrison supported raising tariffs. After his election, Harrison pushed through bills favored by Republicans that increased tariffs. He urged adoption of the Sherman Anti-Trust Act, which limited industrial monopolies. Harrison lost the 1892 election. He died in Indianapolis in 1901.

▲ **An Expanding Union:** *Between 1889 and 1890, six new states were admitted to the Union: North (1) and South (2) Dakota, Idaho (3), Montana (4), Wyoming (5), and Washington (6).*

▲ **The First Lady:** *Caroline Lavinia Scott Harrison (1832–1892) was a witty, gracious hostess who devoted much time to her church and various charities.*

▶ **The Land Rush:** *The Oklahoma land rush of April 22, 1889, marked the high point of the western land boom. On that day settlers claimed two million acres of newly opened land within a matter of hours.*

▼ **The Battle of Wounded Knee:** *In December 1890, many of the Sioux people, including Chief Big Foot, were killed by government troops at Wounded Knee Creek, South Dakota. This ended a period of unrest, which had started with the rise of the Ghost Dance Cult under the leadership of Sitting Bull.*

Chief Sitting Bull

William McKinley
Republican 1897–1901

VICE-PRESIDENTS: GARRET A. HOBART; THEODORE ROOSEVELT

The quiet, religious McKinley stood for conservative government and currency based on the gold standard. He became the third president to be assassinated while in office.

William McKinley was born in 1843 in Niles, Ohio, son of an iron foundry worker. He attended a private school, Poland Seminary, then went on to Allegheny College in Pennsylvania. When poor health forced him to leave, he joined the Union army, where he was promoted to brevet major in 1865. After the war, McKinley studied law and was admitted to the Ohio bar in 1867.

In 1876, McKinley ran for Congress. He served there until 1891, earning a reputation as an advocate of business owners. In 1892, he was elected governor of Ohio and served two terms. In 1896, he was nominated for president and faced a strong opponent in William Jennings Bryan, who represented the working classes. Bryan also supported free coinage of silver. Other Democrats who preferred the gold standard sided with McKinley, whose supporters included Republicans and businesspeople. McKinley won by a narrow victory.

When McKinley took office in 1897, war with Spain seemed imminent. After the U.S. battleship *Maine* was sunk in Havana harbor in 1898, Congress declared war and the United States won a fairly quick victory. Cuba was liberated, although America retained the right to intervene in a crisis. After this victory, the United States was recognized as a world power. Through his support, gold became the official standard for U.S. currency. McKinley was re-elected in 1900. The next September, he was shot by an anarchist while attending the Pan-American Exposition at Buffalo, New York. McKinley was buried in Canton, Ohio.

◀ **The First Lady:** *Ida Saxton McKinley (1847–1907) was an invalid when she became First Lady. Yet she graciously received White House guests while seated in a chair.*

▲ **New Territories:** *Victory in the Spanish-American War gave the U.S. new territories: the Philippines, Guam, and Puerto Rico. Later, the U.S. would pay Spain $20,000,000 for the Philippines.*

▲ **Front Porch Campaign:** *Leading the nation during the "gay nineties," a time of relative prosperity, William McKinley campaigned with the slogan "a full dinner pail," to increase his appeal to working-class Americans, as well as the rich. He also ran a "front porch" campaign, making informal speeches in front of his modest house.*

Theodore Roosevelt
Republican 1901–1909

VICE-PRESIDENT: NONE; CHARLES W. FAIRBANKS

One of the most versatile presidents, Roosevelt was a traveler, writer, naturalist, soldier, sportsman, and politician.

Theodore Roosevelt was born on October 27, 1858, in New York City, into a well-to-do family. As a boy he suffered from asthma but he worked hard to build a muscular, healthy body. After finishing Harvard University in 1880, he attended law school at Columbia but quit to run for state congress. Personal tragedy prompted Roosevelt to leave congress in 1884; both his mother and young wife died on the same day. Roosevelt bought a ranch in North Dakota and moved west with his young daughter. After his father died, he returned to the East.

Under President McKinley, Roosevelt was appointed assistant secretary of the navy. When the Spanish-American War began, he resigned to organize a volunteer cavalry that became known as the Rough Riders. Roosevelt became a national hero after leading a victorious charge up Kettle Hill in San Juan, Puerto Rico.

In 1898, he ran for governor of New York and won. The Republican party named him vice-presidential candidate in 1900. Fate made Roosevelt president when McKinley was shot in 1901. From that day until 1909, Roosevelt promoted his "Square Deal" reform legislation and worked for peace through diplomacy, earning a Nobel Peace prize for his efforts. In 1907, a Monetary Commission was established, which became the basis for the Federal Reserve system.

After two eventful terms, Roosevelt left office. He retired to a life of travel, writing, and lecturing. Roosevelt died in his sleep in Oyster Bay, New York, in 1919.

◀ **The First Lady:** *Edith Kermit Carow Roosevelt (1861–1948) was a cultured, scholarly, and sensible woman. The couple married in 1886 and had five children.*

▲ **Preserving America:** *Believing that speculative interests were eroding America's natural resources, Roosevelt set aside vast wilderness lands for conservation. These later became part of the country's national parks and nature reserves.*

▼ **The Panama Canal:** *In 1903, Roosevelt negotiated an agreement with Panama that resulted in the completion of the Panama Canal 10 years later.*

▶ **Kitty Hawk:** *On December 17, 1903, Orville and Wilbur Wright made the first controlled airplane flight at Kill Devil Hill, near Kitty Hawk, North Carolina.*

William Howard Taft

Republican 1909–1913

VICE-PRESIDENT: JAMES S. SHERMAN

No other president held more important government posts than William Taft. His conservative approach and quiet ways were a distinct contrast to his exuberant predecessor, Theodore Roosevelt.

William Howard Taft was born on September 15, 1857, in Cincinnati, Ohio, to a wealthy family. He graduated from Yale University in 1878 and from the Cincinnati Law School in 1880. Seven years later, he became a judge of the superior court of Ohio, and in 1890, was appointed solicitor-general in President Harrison's administration. From 1892 to 1900, Taft served as a judge on the U.S. Sixth Circuit Court of Appeals. In 1900, he became civil governor of the Philippines where he set up a judicial system and developed schools, roads, post offices, and banks. He became secretary of war under Roosevelt in 1904 and then temporary governor of Cuba in 1906.

Supported by Roosevelt when he left office, Taft was elected president in 1908. He gradually lost the support of liberal Republicans by following a more conservative course. He did follow Roosevelt's lead in "trust-busting" (breaking up large corporate monopolies) by dissolving Standard Oil and the tobacco trusts. He worked for world peace and reciprocal treaties. As foreign nations cooperated with U.S. policies, the United States rewarded them with financial investments.

After losing the 1912 election, Taft became a professor of constitutional law at Yale University. In 1921, he was appointed chief justice of the Supreme Court. He served on the Court until 1930, shortly before he died.

▶ **The First Lady:** *Helen Herron Taft (1861–1943) and her "Will" shared many intellectual and musical interests when they wed in 1886. An eager traveler, she willingly took her three children to live in different countries when Taft was assigned to govern there.*

▲ **Parcel Post:** *The U.S. parcel post system started in 1912, during Taft's administration.*

▶ **Income Tax:** *Congress approved the Sixteenth and Seventeenth Amendments, providing for the levying of an income tax and the election of senators by popular vote.*

◀ **The Growing Union:** *Two new states, New Mexico(1) and Arizona (2), joined the Union in 1912.*

Woodrow Wilson
Democrat 1913–1921

VICE-PRESIDENT: THOMAS R. MARSHALL

Wilson tried to keep America out of World War I, then worked to rebuild international goodwill when that war ended. As president, he said his main duty was "to look out for the general interests of the country."

Born Thomas Woodrow Wilson in 1856 in Staunton, Virginia, he had a happy homelife and fine education. After graduating from Princeton University in New Jersey, Wilson studied law at the University of Virginia. He then became a teacher, majoring in political science and legal studies at Johns Hopkins University. He taught at Bryn Mawr, at Wesleyan University, and finally at Princeton, where he became president. In 1910, he ran as a Democrat for governor of New Jersey. His winning platform emphasized individualism.

In 1913, he became U.S. president, defeating a split Republican party. Wilson called his program the New Freedom. He passed key financial legislation and established the Federal Trade Commission. Wilson worked to keep America out of World War I, which had begun in Europe in 1914. In 1917, as his second term began, Germany threatened to attack American ships. Wilson asked Congress to declare war, saying, "The world must be made safe for democracy."

After Germany's defeat, Wilson led a delegation to the 1918 Peace Conference and proposed his Fourteen Points program. One part was a League of Nations, where nations could debate and try to avoid war. During the rest of his term, he was in poor health and his second wife, Edith, helped him to carry on his work. Wilson died in Washington, D.C., in 1924.

▶ **The First Lady:** *Edith Bolling Galt Wilson (1872–1961) married Wilson in 1915 when both were widowed. A distant relative of Native American princess Pocahontas, she later wrote her memoirs and attended John F. Kennedy's inauguration.*

▼ **The World's Tallest Building:** *The 60-story Woolworth building appeared on the New York skyline in 1913. Designed in Gothic style, it soared to 792 feet and was heralded as the tallest building in the world.*

▲ **The Sinking of the Lusitania:** *In 1915, a German U-boat sunk the unarmed British liner* Lusitania *with the loss of 1,195 lives, 128 of whom were Americans. The event outraged the United States.*

◀ **Votes for Women:** *In 1920, during Wilson's second term, the 20th Amendment to the Constitution gave women the right to vote.*

Warren G. Harding

Republican 1921–1923

VICE-PRESIDENT: CALVIN COOLIDGE

During his presidential campaign, Harding urged Americans to seek healing and normalcy, but his administration was tainted by the corruption of high officials.

The first of eight children, Warren Harding was born in 1865 on a farm in Corsica, Ohio. He worked on the farm and attended rural schools. At 14, Harding entered Ohio Central College and graduated in only three years. In Marion, Ohio, Harding became a typesetter, then editor, at a local newspaper. In 1884, he borrowed $300 and bought the Marion *Daily Star*. He and his wife, whom he married in 1891, made the *Star* an influential paper. In 1899, he was elected to the Ohio senate for the first of two terms. After his second term, in 1903, he became lieutenant governor. Elected to the U.S. Senate in 1914, he served on the Committee on Foreign Relations.

In 1920, Harding was nominated for president. Republican leaders agreed that his unblemished reputation and presidential looks might lead to victory. In 1921, he met with leaders of six European nations, Japan, and China to limit naval armaments and discuss the Far East. The U.S. government became more businesslike after Congress approved a budget system. Harding also urged an increase in federal jobs when the unemployment rate rose. In the summer of 1923, Harding set out to tour the West. He died in San Francisco while still in office. He was buried in Marion, Ohio.

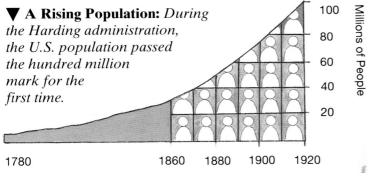

▼ **A Rising Population:** *During the Harding administration, the U.S. population passed the hundred million mark for the first time.*

Millions of People

100
80
60
40
20

1780   1860   1880   1900   1920

▶ **The First Lady:** *Florence Kling DeWolfe Harding (1860–1924), a self-reliant banker's daughter, taught piano lessons before marrying Harding. As First Lady, she entertained often and traveled with her husband.*

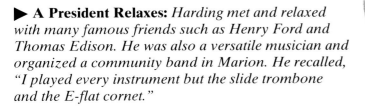

▶ **A President Relaxes:** *Harding met and relaxed with many famous friends such as Henry Ford and Thomas Edison. He was also a versatile musician and organized a community band in Marion. He recalled, "I played every instrument but the slide trombone and the E-flat cornet."*

Calvin Coolidge
Republican 1923–1929

VICE-PRESIDENT: NONE; CHARLES G. DAWES

The Coolidge era was prosperous. New inventions and industries made life easier. In contrast to his sociable predecessor, "Silent Cal" was a quiet, serious man who refused a third term by saying simply, "I do not choose to run."

Calvin Coolidge was born in 1872 in Plymouth, Vermont. He graduated in 1895 from Amherst College. For ten years he practiced law, before serving on the Massachusetts General Court. Steadily, he moved toward higher office and, in 1912, entered the state senate. From 1916 to 1918, Coolidge was lieutenant governor of Massachusetts. While governor (1918–1922), he gained national publicity when he settled the 1919 Boston police strike. He was vice-president on the 1920 ticket and became president in 1923, upon Harding's death.

Coolidge sought to limit government and stay out of foreign affairs. After using the government surplus to reduce the national debt, he cut taxes and won fresh popularity. Still, farmers objected when Coolidge vetoed bills for farm relief. Coolidge was re-elected in 1924. Again he cut taxes, then supported a flood control bill. In foreign affairs, he foresaw the failure of the Kellogg-Briand Pact to outlaw war. Coolidge said that "a complete and satisfying life" was only possible when people followed laws based on righteousness. He remarked, "Parchment will fail, the sword will fail, it is only the spiritual nature of man that can be triumphant."

He died after retiring from office, at his home in 1933.

▲ **The First Lady:** *Grace Anna Goodhue Coolidge (1879–1957) taught at a school for the deaf after finishing college. Much more sociable than her husband, this sports-loving mother of two sons became one of Washington's most popular hostesses.*

▲ **Better Transportation:** *An era of rapid change in transportation, aviators crossed the Atlantic Ocean, while the U.S. auto industry produced more and safer cars.*

▶ **Radios and Motion Pictures:** *During the Coolidge era, new forms of communication spread as radios became part of American homes. Motion pictures with sound came to movie theaters, and telephones connected America and Europe.*

▶ **Modern Appliances:** *Newly devised electrical appliances made their way into the home in the 1920s, including stoves, ovens, heaters, irons, kettles, and refrigerators.*

Herbert Hoover

Republican 1929–1933

VICE-PRESIDENT: CHARLES CURTIS

Hoover was among the most experienced of presidents, but his term was marred by the worst economic depression in U.S. history. Herbert Hoover was born in 1874 in West Branch, Iowa. In 1895, he graduated from Stanford University, in California, and became a mining engineer. From 1901 to 1914, he headed a successful British engineering firm. During World War I, Hoover helped Americans get out of Europe, then organized a food-relief project. Later, he directed the U.S. Food Administration, which fed the Allies while avoiding food shortages in America. Hoover's postwar work as head of the American Relief Administration saved millions of lives.

He easily won the 1928 presidential race and looked forward to fulfilling his campaign pledge of "two chickens in every pot and a car in every garage." Hoover promoted a Federal Farm Board and the Smoot-Hawley Act, one of the highest tariff bills ever written. In October 1929, the U.S. economy began to plummet. A world war and speculative buying of stocks in America had contributed to disaster. Nations could not repay loans to the U.S., nor buy American goods.

There was a surge of factory closings, bank failures, and job losses. To try to end the depression, Hoover approved banking reforms, federal loans to businesses, unemployment relief, and a strict federal budget. He also asked Congress for more farm relief and public works. However, Americans sought new solutions. They elected Franklin Roosevelt in a landslide victory in 1932.

Later, Truman asked Hoover to head the Famine Emergency Fund, after World War II, and the Hoover Commission. The latter found ways to make the executive branch of government more effective. Hoover died in New York City in 1964.

▶ **Life-Saving Mission:** *In 1900, during the Boxer Rebellion, Herbert and Lou Hoover assisted a relief effort, working in hospitals and building barricades to protect a village. Hoover risked his life to save Chinese children.*

▼ **The Wall Street Crash:** *Panic swept through New York as rumors spread about the falling value of stocks and shares. Thousands crowded onto Wall Street to hear the latest news.*

▲ **The First Lady:** *Lou Henry Hoover (1874–1944), also a Stanford graduate, raised two sons while living in more than 12 countries. As First Lady, she entertained at her own expense and made many public appearances. Her husband called her "a symbol of everything wholesome."*

▼ **The Hoover Dam:** *In 1931, construction began on the Boulder (now Hoover) Dam, located between Nevada and Arizona. Hoover's administration also expanded the national parks and forests by millions of acres.*

Franklin D. Roosevelt

Democrat 1933–1945

VICE-PRESIDENTS: JOHN N. GARNER; HENRY A. WALLACE; HARRY S. TRUMAN

"The only thing we have to fear is fear itself," Roosevelt told Americans after his election. He led America out of the Great Depression and through the largest world war in history.

Franklin Delano Roosevelt, an only child, was born on January 30, 1882, in Hyde Park, New York. Theodore Roosevelt was his fifth cousin. At 14, Roosevelt entered Groton, a preparatory school, in Massachusetts. He graduated from Harvard in 1904 and finished Columbia Law School three years later. In 1905, he married his sixth cousin, Anna Eleanor Roosevelt. He was elected to the New York senate in 1910, after a brief law career. Three years later, Roosevelt became assistant secretary of the navy. In 1921, he was stricken with polio. Roosevelt spent several years exercising to regain his strength but could never walk again without metal leg braces. Re-entering public life, Roosevelt was elected governor of New York in 1928 and 1930. Running for president in 1932, "F.D.R." swept the election.

During a special "Hundred Days" session of Congress, Roosevelt asked for extra authority to ease the economic crisis of the depression. He set out to regulate credit, banking, foreign exchange, and currency. He created the National Recovery Administration to regulate and raise wages. Congress approved money for home loans, shortened working hours, discouraged child labor, and tried to eliminate unfair methods of competition. Then came additional farm relief and the Civilian Conservation Corps, which employed 500,000 young men in reforestation projects. The Social Security Act of 1935 was also set up to provide financial aid for the elderly. Roosevelt had hoped to balance the national budget, but the debt grew during these years.

► **The First Lady:** *Anna Eleanor Roosevelt Roosevelt (1884–1962) was known as a dynamic advocate for the disadvantaged. She entertained, as had traditional First Ladies, wrote a newspaper column, gave speeches and lectures, and traveled abroad as a goodwill ambassador. She also served as spokesperson for the United Nations.*

▲ **Dust Bowls:** *The mid-1930s were marked by a series of droughts in the midwest. This, combined with overfarming, led to barren "dust bowls" where the topsoil blew away. Thousands of farmers migrated to California and the Southwest.*

Roosevelt continued his programs after being re-elected in 1936. Late in 1937, he met with business leaders, hoping to stave off another economic crisis. Congress approved loans to industry, low cost housing, and projects for flood control and federal buildings.

When World War II began in Europe in 1939, Roosevelt supported Britain and France. He kept America out of the war until the Japanese bombed the U.S. naval base at Pearl Harbor, Hawaii, in 1941. Once in the war, Roosevelt mobilized factory production of military arms and equipment. He also played a leading part in creating an alliance with Britain and the Soviet Union. He worked closely with other Allied leaders, meeting with them at a series of conferences. Roosevelt was elected to a record fourth term in 1944. He died on April 12, 1945.

▶ **Soup Kitchens:** *Soup kitchens for the poor and unemployed were very familiar in the 1930s. In spite of aid given by the federal government to American industry, the economy did not improve greatly during the early years of Roosevelt's New Deal.*

▼ **Pearl Harbor:** *When Japanese planes bombed the Pacific Fleet's Hawaiian base at Pearl Harbor, many people lost their lives. Two days later, the U.S. declared war on Japan.*

▲ **Golden Gate Bridge:** *When the Golden Gate Bridge opened in May, 1937, 200,000 people crossed it to celebrate the occasion. It was the longest suspension bridge in the world, measuring 6,450 feet.*

▲ **Mount Rushmore:** *In 1941, work was finally completed on one of America's most famous monuments — Mount Rushmore. The faces of Washington, Jefferson, Theodore Roosevelt, and Lincoln were immortalized in the rock of the South Dakotan mountainside.*

▲ **The Yalta Conference:** *During the war years, Roosevelt held a series of meetings with other Allied leaders. At the 1945 Yalta Conference with Churchill and Stalin, victory in Europe was already assured.*

Harry S. Truman

Democrat 1945–1953

VICE-PRESIDENT: NONE; ALBEN W. BARKLEY

A sign on Harry Truman's desk read, "The buck stops here." As president, Truman knew he had the last word on major decisions — and the praise or blame that might follow. Rarely has any world leader faced such critical choices as those Truman had to make.

Harry S. Truman was born in Lamar, Missouri, on May 8, 1884. After high school, he became a bank clerk, then spent twelve years farming. Truman had no money for college, but he read widely. In World War I, he served as an artillery battery captain in France and was praised for leadership and bravery.

Back home, he wed his childhood sweetheart and opened a men's clothing business. It failed during the economic slump of the early 1920s. He was twice elected county judge, then Missouri sent him to the U.S. Senate in 1934. Truman became known as an honest, hardworking senator who spearheaded reforms in America's transportation system. In 1944, he became President Franklin D. Roosevelt's running mate. On April 2, 1945, Roosevelt died. After just three months as vice-president, Truman was now president. "I felt as if the moon, the stars, and all the planets had fallen on me," he later said.

In May, the Allied forces won the war in Europe, but the war against Japan raged on. Told by advisors that millions might die if the war continued, Truman agreed to drop two atomic bombs on Japan. Japan surrendered a few days later. Afterwards, Truman had to deal with the Soviet Union, which began testing its own atomic weapons in 1949. The Korean War began in 1950. In 1953, Truman retired to Missouri. The popular former president died in 1972, at age 88.

▼ **The First Lady**: *Elizabeth Virginia (Bess) Wallace Truman (1885–1982), a friendly and supportive First Lady, was called "the Boss" by her affectionate husband.*

▼ **Civil Rights**: *In the 1940s, Truman was an early advocate of more rights and opportunities for black Americans. Despite criticism from southern Democrats and others, he did not change his position.*

▼ **Fair Deal**: *Truman's 1948 Fair Deal program included a Fair Employment Practices Act and plans for slum clearance, public housing, full employment, and national health insurance.*

◀ **Atomic Bombs**: *Truman said he felt a "terrible responsibility" for the suffering atomic bombs caused in Hiroshima and Nagasaki, Japan. Yet he believed they had saved millions of lives on both sides.*

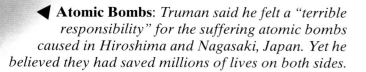

Dwight D. Eisenhower
Republican 1953–1961

VICE-PRESIDENT: RICHARD M. NIXON

A military hero, Eisenhower served as president during prosperous times. Upon leaving office, he called America "the strongest, most influential, and most productive nation in the world."

Dwight David Eisenhower was born in 1890 in Texas, and raised in Abilene, Kansas. A talented student, he graduated from West Point in 1915, then served in Houston, Texas. In 1918, Eisenhower became commander of a tank training center in Pennsylvania. He then served in the Panama Canal Zone until 1924. Varied jobs under outstanding commanders prepared him for leadership. He was General Douglas MacArthur's aide and went with him to the Philippines in 1935. The supreme commander of Allied forces in Europe, Eisenhower helped to plan the D-Day invasion of Normandy in 1944.

After the war, Eisenhower served as president of Columbia University and later as supreme commander of the Northern Atlantic Treaty Organization (NATO). Both parties wanted him to run for president in 1952. He led the Republicans to victory.

In domestic affairs, Eisenhower approved more Social Security benefits and a higher minimum wage. His administration created the Department of Health, Education, and Welfare. Abroad, he confronted the spread of communism. American competition with Russia over the building of new nuclear weapons and space exploration was called the Cold War.

Eisenhower was re-elected in 1956. Voters echoed the slogan, "We like Ike." The U.S. broke diplomatic ties with Cuba after a communist government took control. Eisenhower supported the wise use of military power and the quest for world peace. A popular elder statesman, he retired to his farm in Pennsylvania. He died in 1969.

Sputnik

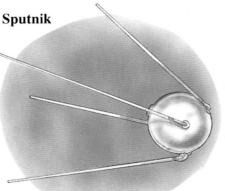

◀ **The Space Race:** *In 1957, the Soviet Union launched the space satellite,* Sputnik. *American scientists achieved this feat in 1958 with the* Explorer I. *A "space race" between the two nations continued through the 1960s.*

▲ **The First Lady:** *Mamie Geneva Doud Eisenhower (1896–1979) was an accomplished hostess and traveled widely. Their leadership role in the U.S. and access to air travel meant that the Eisenhowers made more trips and received more diplomatic visitors than any past administration.*

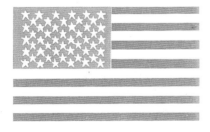

▲ **McDonald's Arrives:** *In 1954, Ray Kroc began to sell the McDonald's hamburger franchises.*

◀ **Fifty States:** *In 1959, Alaska and Hawaii became part of the Union. The American flag now had 50 stars!*

John F. Kennedy

Democrat 1961–1963

VICE-PRESIDENT: LYNDON B. JOHNSON

The Kennedy administration held a vision to move America forward. The youngest person ever elected president, Kennedy was also the first Catholic to hold the office.

John Fitzgerald Kennedy was born on May 29, 1917, in Brookline, Massachusetts. He was the second of nine children belonging to a wealthy, Irish-American family. He suffered many illnesses during his youth, but his charm and speaking skill led classmates at Choate Academy to vote him "most likely to succeed" in 1935. At Harvard, he studied economics and government. He graduated with honors.

During World War II, Kennedy was commanding a navy PT boat in the Solomon Islands when it was sunk in 1943. He received the U.S. Navy and Marine Corps medal and Purple Heart for helping to rescue the crew.

Kennedy ran for Congress from Massachusetts in 1946. In Washington, he supported Truman's programs for workers' rights, and benefits for veterans and the elderly. He became a Senator in 1952, then ran for president in 1960.

As president, Kennedy supported antipoverty programs and civil rights legislation for black Americans. In 1961, he authorized a failed invasion by exiled Cubans to overthrow dictator Fidel Castro. The next year, he ordered the Soviet government to dismantle its missile sites on Cuba. Around the world, people waited fearfully until the U.S.S.R. agreed. Kennedy led the 1963 Nuclear Test Ban Treaty, which forbade testing atomic bombs in space, the atmosphere, and the seas. He spoke hopefully of America's future. Kennedy was assassinated in Dallas, Texas, on November 22, 1963, before he could realize his vision for world peace.

◀ **The First Lady:** *Jacqueline Lee Bouvier Kennedy Onassis (1929–1994) brought youth and elegance to the White House and restored its public rooms. In 1968, she married Greek businessman Aristotle Onassis (who died in 1975), and later became a respected book editor in New York City.*

◀ **Racial Equality:** *To show his support for civil rights, Kennedy sent federal marshals to stop the violence in newly integrated southern schools.*

▼ **The Peace Corps:** *In 1961, with his brother-in-law Sargent Shriver, Kennedy founded the Peace Corps. By the 1990s, more than 6,000 Americans worked in 90 countries, helping with local projects such as education, farming, construction, and health care.*

GO IN PEACE
Join the Peace Corps

▲ **The First Astronauts:** *Russian Yuri Gagarin became the first man in space, adding further fuel to America's space race. The following year, in 1962, John Glenn (see above) became the first American astronaut to orbit the earth in space.*

Lyndon B. Johnson
Democrat 1963–1969

VICE-PRESIDENT: NONE; HUBERT H. HUMPHREY

After Kennedy's death, President Johnson told a shocked, grieving nation, "Let us continue." He pushed Kennedy's last proposals through Congress and launched his own Great Society program.

Lyndon Baines Johnson was born in 1908 in Stonewall, Texas. He paid his way through Southwest Texas State College, graduating in 1930. He was deeply concerned about poverty, and during the Great Depression he administered a state program to help young people find jobs. In 1937, Johnson was elected to the House of Representatives and served five terms, interrupted by service in the navy during World War II. In 1948, he was elected to the Senate; five years later he became the youngest minority leader ever. The next year, with the Senate Democrats in power, he became majority leader. Bright, friendly, and skilled in politics, he worked well with people in both parties to pass legislation.

After Kennedy's assassination, Johnson worked to pass further civil rights bills. He cut the government budget and reduced income taxes. Re-elected by a landslide in 1964, he introduced his Great Society plan. Johnson called for a War on Poverty, including job training, health care for the elderly and the poor, and aid to education. The war in Vietnam, fought against the Communist regime, cast a dark shadow over Johnson's social programs. By March 1968, the debate over Vietnam was so bitter that Johnson announced he would not run again, but would devote his time to ending the war. Peace talks began the next year as Johnson retired to his *LBJ Ranch* in Texas. He died in 1973.

▶ **The Moon Walk:** *In 1968, three U.S. astronauts orbited the moon. Johnson praised them for taking "all of us, all over the world, into a new era." The following year, Neil Armstrong became the first man to walk on the moon.*

▶ **The First Lady:** *Claudia Alta (Lady Bird) Taylor Johnson (1912–), promoted the care and beautification of America's environment. She also took an active part in politics and the antipoverty program.*

◀ **Martin Luther King:** *The civil rights leader, Dr. Martin Luther King, Jr., was assassinated in 1968. A Baptist preacher, King had inspired his followers to take nonviolent action against racial discrimination.*

Richard M. Nixon

Republican 1969–1974

VICE-PRESIDENTS: SPIRO T. AGNEW; GERALD R. FORD

"Bring us together," read signs carried by voters during the 1968 election. When Nixon won that race, he faced a nation deeply divided over an unpopular war.

Richard Milhous Nixon was born in 1913 in Yorba Linda, California. From humble beginnings, he worked and studied hard. He completed studies at Whittier College and Duke University Law School. He served as a navy officer in the Pacific during World War II and in 1947 was elected to Congress. In 1950, he became a U.S. Senator. In 1952, Eisenhower chose him as vice-president. Nixon took an active part in foreign diplomacy and domestic affairs during those eight years. After losing the 1960 presidential election by only 113,000 votes, Nixon ran for governor of California, but also lost. In 1968, he won the presidential election. Gradually, Nixon withdrew U.S. troops from Vietnam and worked towards an end to that war. He stressed foreign affairs, discussing arms limitation with the Soviet Union and encouraging peace talks within the Middle East. Re-elected in 1972, Nixon faced a political scandal. The press discovered that top White House officials had hired men to burglarize and wiretap the Democratic National Committee offices at the Watergate Hotel in Washington, D.C. A Senate investigative committee suspected Nixon of trying to cover up the Watergate affair. He resigned from office, saying that this was the best way to begin "the healing process."

The new president, Gerald Ford, pardoned Nixon for any offenses he may have committed. No legal action was taken against him. Nixon retired to California, where he wrote and gave interviews on foreign policy. He died in 1994 at age 81.

▼ **"Red China":** *Nixon restored relations with the People's Republic of China, making an historic visit there in 1972. The trip was a diplomatic triumph for the president.*

▲ **The First Lady:** *Thelma Catherine (Pat) Ryan Nixon (1912–1993) was a self-made person like her husband. She promoted the spirit of volunteerism and made many official foreign trips, including solo ones.*

◄ **The Soviet Connection:** *In 1959, as vice-president, Nixon had heated debates with Soviet leader Nikita S. Krushchev. He received international attention for his firm stance. Later, in 1972, Nixon signed trade agreements and an arms treaty with the Soviet General Secretary, Leonid Brezhnev.*

Gerald R. Ford

Republican 1974–1977

VICE-PRESIDENT: NELSON A. ROCKEFELLER

At a time when many Americans mistrusted government, Ford's honest reputation restored confidence. Just months before, he had been chosen to replace vice-president Spiro Agnew, who had resigned. Then, he succeeded Nixon, the first president ever to resign.

Gerald R. Ford was born in 1913 in Omaha, Nebraska, and grew up in Grand Rapids, Michigan. At the University of Michigan, he played football, then coached the game while attending Yale Law School. He served as a lieutenant commander in the navy during World War II, then returned to Michigan to practice law.

Ford was elected to Congress in 1948, where he served for 25 years. He was Senate Minority Leader for the last eight years. In 1973, he stepped in as vice-president, when the former vice-president resigned after being accused of bribery. After the Watergate scandal broke, President Richard Nixon resigned from office in August, 1974.

On becoming president, Ford said it was "an hour of history that troubles our minds and hurts our hearts." He granted Nixon a full pardon, saying that the nation must set aside the Watergate episode and move forward. Ford faced rising inflation and a sluggish economy. He promoted economic programs to stimulate jobs. He also tried to reduce government controls on businesses.

Ford lost the 1976 election and retired to write his memoirs. He lectured widely on the presidency and public affairs. He and his popular wife, Betty, are also involved in charitable and sports events.

▶ **The First Lady:** *Elizabeth Bloomer (Betty) Ford (1918–) became known as one of the most forthright of all First Ladies. She lent support to the Equal Rights Amendment for women, and founded the Betty Ford Clinic for people with substance abuse problems.*

◀ **The Middle East:** *The Ford administration urged Prime Minister Begin of Israel (top left) and President Sadat of Egypt (bottom left) to continue the truce they had agreed upon during Nixon's term in office.*

▲ **The Vietnam War:** *The Vietnam War finally came to an end in 1975, when the South Vietnamese forces surrendered to the Communist Vietcong. Thousands of Vietnamese were airlifted out by military helicopters.*

Jimmy Carter

Democrat 1977–1981

VICE-PRESIDENT: WALTER F. MONDALE

Throughout his life, Jimmy Carter campaigned for human rights at home and abroad. Few presidents have been so active and admired for their contributions after leaving office.

James Earl Carter was born in 1924 in Plains, Georgia. As a child, he took part in the family peanut-growing business. After attending a junior college and Georgia Tech, he went to the U.S. Naval Academy at Annapolis, Maryland, where he finished 59th in a class of 820. In 1946, shortly after marrying his hometown sweetheart, Carter began a series of navy assignments that took him to several bases. He returned to Plains to run the family business after his father died. In 1962, Carter entered politics. He began as a Georgia state senator, then in 1970, after a second attempt, he was elected governor. Other governors credited Carter for using business principles to make government more efficient. He also turned his attention to civil rights and the environment. Still, the American public did not know Carter well when he began running for the presidency in 1974. During a two-year campaign, he worked hard to meet voters. He also made many television appearances to explain his goals for America.

As president, Carter created many new jobs and reduced unemployment. Yet soaring crude oil prices fanned inflation. After he lost re-election in 1980, the Carters returned to Plains to write books, lecture, and take part in their church. They developed new projects, such as Habitat for Humanity, an organization that builds homes for needy people around the world.

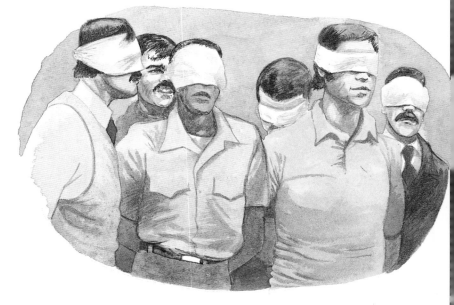

▲ **The Hostage Crisis:** *In 1979, revolutionary students stormed the U.S. embassy in Tehran, Iran, and took 63 American hostages. Although the hostages were finally released in January, 1980, Carter's mishandling of the crisis helped lead to his downfall in the following election.*

▲ **The First Lady:** *Rosalynn Smith Carter (1927–), a hard-working mother of four, managed parts of the family peanut business. She also spearheaded projects to help the elderly and mentally ill.*

▲ **Grain Embargo:** *Carter halted the delivery of grain to Russia in protest at the Soviet invasion of Afghanistan.*

Ronald Reagan

Republican 1981–1989

VICE-PRESIDENT: GEORGE BUSH

Known as "the great communicator," Ronald Reagan's conservative approach appealed to many who thought the federal government had grown too large and expensive.

Reagan was born in 1911 in Tampeco, Illinois. He worked his way through Eureka College, graduating in 1932. After working as a radio sports announcer, he went to Hollywood and became a well-known actor. He took an interest in politics, and by 1962 Reagan firmly believed that government should trim its budget and bureaucracy. He became governor of California in 1966 and tried to implement his ideas. However, the state legislature, controlled by Democrats, made it hard for him to reduce local government and cut taxes.

▶ **The First Lady:** *Nancy Davis Reagan (1923–) was an actress before her marriage and brought elegant style to the White House. She promoted favorite causes, including drug education and a foster grandparents program.*

◀ **Irangate:** *In 1986, it was revealed that the Reagan administration had shipped arms to Iran, against official policy, to try to gain the release of American hostages. Money made from the deal had been used to support the contra rebels in Nicaragua. The subsequent investigation caused many problems for the Reagan administration.*

▶ **Glasnost:** *In 1987 and 1988, Reagan signed two historic agreements with the Soviet Union (Russia) to eliminate some medium-range and shorter-range missiles. It heralded the end of the cold war and the beginning of "glasnost" or openness.*

During his 1980 presidential election, Reagan used television to reach voters. In one debate, he asked the people to consider the question, "Are you better off than you were four years ago?" High interest rates and high inflation led many Americans to choose Reagan that year. He also attracted voters who believed the U.S. needed to build more arms. Congress supported some of Reagan's programs, including cuts in taxes and domestic spending. Yet increased military spending meant that the Federal deficit continued to rise. During his second term, in 1985, Reagan held an important meeting with the Soviet Union's leader, Mikhail Gorbachev. This led to better relations between the two nations and to reductions in nuclear weapons. Since leaving office, Reagan has campaigned for other Republican candidates.

George Bush
Republican 1989–1993

VICE-PRESIDENT: DAN QUAYLE

Born into wealth, George Bush could have led a life of quiet comfort but instead chose to devote himself to public service. A leader since his youth, Bush believes strongly in the values of service, religion, and family.

George Bush was born in 1924 in Milton, Massachusetts. During World War II, Bush became the youngest pilot in the U.S. Navy, surviving some dangerous missions in the South Pacific. Back home, he married Barbara Bush and attended Yale University. After graduating, he went to Texas and worked his way up in the oil business.

In 1964, he lost his quest for a U.S. Senate seat but was elected to Congress in 1966. He became ambassador to the United Nations under President Nixon in 1971. Three years later, he became head of the Republican National Committee. In 1976, Bush became chief U.S. envoy in Beijing. He then moved back to America to become head of the Central Intelligence Agency (CIA). In 1978, he was chosen as vice-presidential candidate on the 1980 Reagan ticket.

When Reagan's two terms ended, Bush was elected president and pledged to "build a better America." During his term, Bush met with Russian leaders to discuss the removal of troops from Eastern Europe. Bush also promoted a bill to guarantee rights for disabled Americans and signed the Clean Air Act in 1990. That same year, he sent U.S. troops to the Persian Gulf. The troops joined with United Nations forces and made Iraq abandon its invasion of Kuwait.

After losing the 1992 election, the Bushes returned to Texas to write, campaign for friends, and enjoy private family life.

▶ **The First Lady:** *Barbara Pierce Bush (1925–) founded the Barbara Bush Foundation for Family Literacy, one of her favorite causes. Her natural, friendly ways made her an extremely popular First Lady.*

◀ **Fair Housing:** *As a congressman from Texas, Bush voted for the Fair Housing Act of 1968, which allowed people of any race to live where they chose.*

▼ **Operation Desert Storm:** *A U.S. and United Nations offensive forced Iraq to end its invasion of Kuwait.*

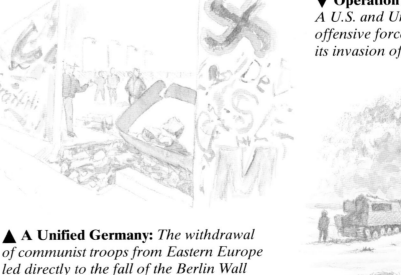

▲ **A Unified Germany:** *The withdrawal of communist troops from Eastern Europe led directly to the fall of the Berlin Wall and the unification of Germany.*

Bill Clinton
Democrat 1993–

Vice-President: Albert Gore, Jr.

Change swept the air as Clinton moved to Washington in 1989. He was the first president born after World War II, part of the "baby boom" generation.

Born William Jefferson Blythe IV, in 1946 in Hope, Arkansas, Clinton was named for his father, who had died a few months earlier. His mother, Virginia, worked hard to become a nurse anesthetist and care for her son. Clinton later took his stepfather's last name. He was an outstanding student, who played the saxophone and led many groups. Chosen to attend Boys' Nation in 1963, he met President Kennedy at the White House, who inspired him.

Through jobs, scholarships, and loans, Clinton attended Georgetown University. From 1968 to 1969, he was a Rhodes scholar at Oxford University, in England, then studied law at Yale. There he met a brilliant fellow student, Hillary Rodham, whom he would marry in 1975. Clinton refused well paying jobs at large law firms and returned to Arkansas to teach. At age 28, he ran for state congress but lost. In 1976, he was elected state attorney general. Clinton became governor two years later, when he was only 32. During five terms as governor, Clinton stressed job creation, health care, and programs to improve child welfare. He carried out broad education reforms. In 1991, the nation's governors voted Clinton the most effective governor.

After a vigorous campaign, Clinton won the presidential election in 1992. Taking office, he appointed a Health Care Task Force. He worked on an anticrime bill, welfare reform, and programs to aid the economy. Cheerful and energetic, Clinton set out to help the United States meet the challenges of the 21st century.

▼ **NAFTA:** *The North American Free Trade Agreement reduces trade barriers between the U.S., Mexico, and Canada, and will later include South America. NAFTA is unpopular with U.S. trade unions, who fear job losses to the poorer nations. Yet it will secure the Americas as the largest free trading block in the world.*

▲ **The First Lady:** *Hillary Rodham Clinton (1947–) was named one of the 100 most influential attorneys in America. As First Lady, she has key jobs in health care reform and other projects, along with her duties as wife, mother, and hostess.*

▶ **The Inauguration:** *In his inaugural speech, Clinton challenged Americans to "reinvent America" by service and sacrifice.*

Canada

United States

Mexico

Central America
South America

The Presidents

and Vice-Presidents

1. George Washington: *Federalist* 1789–1797. *Vice-president*: John Adams.

2. John Adams: *Federalist* 1797–1801. *Vice-president*: Thomas Jefferson.

3. Thomas Jefferson: *Democratic-Republican* 1801–1809. *Vice-presidents*: Aaron Burr 1801–1805; George Clinton 1805–1809.

4. James Madison: *Democratic-Republican* 1809–1817. *Vice-presidents*: George Clinton 1809–1812; Elbridge Gerry 1813–1814.

5. James Monroe: *Democratic-Republican* 1817–1825. *Vice-president*: Daniel D. Tompkins.

6. John Quincy Adams: *Democratic-Republican* 1825–1829. *Vice-president*: John C. Calhoun.

7. Andrew Jackson: *Democrat* 1829–1837. *Vice-presidents*: John C. Calhoun 1829–1832; Martin Van Buren 1833–1837.

8. Martin Van Buren: *Democrat* 1837–1841. *Vice-president*: Richard M. Johnson.

9. William H. Harrison: *Whig* March–April 1841. *Vice-president*: John Tyler.

10. John Tyler: *Whig* 1841–1845. *Vice-president*: None, as Tyler succeeded Harrison after his death.

11. James K. Polk: *Democrat* 1845–1849. *Vice-president*: George M. Dallas.

12. Zachary Taylor: *Whig* 1849–1850. *Vice-president*: Millard Fillmore.

13. Millard Fillmore: *Whig* 1850–1853. *Vice-president*: None, as Fillmore succeeded Taylor after his death.

14. Franklin Pierce: *Democrat* 1853–1857. *Vice-president*: William R. King.

15. James Buchanan: *Democrat* 1857–1861. *Vice-president*: John C. Breckinridge.

16. Abraham Lincoln: *Republican* 1861–1865. *Vice-presidents*: Hannibal Hamlin 1861–1864; Andrew Johnson 1865.

17. Andrew Johnson: *Democrat* 1865–1869. *Vice-president*: None, as Johnson succeeded Lincoln after his death.

18. Ulysses S. Grant: *Republican* 1869–1877. *Vice-presidents*: Schuyler Colfax 1869–1873; Henry Wilson 1873–1875.

19. Rutherford B. Hayes: *Republican* 1877–1881. *Vice-president*: William A. Wheeler.

20. James A. Garfield: *Republican* March–September 1881. *Vice-president*: Chester A. Arthur.

21. Chester A. Arthur: *Republican* 1881–1885. *Vice-president*: None, as Arthur succeeded Garfield after his death.

22. and **24**. Grover Cleveland: *Democrat* 1885–1889; 1893–1897. *Vice-presidents*: Thomas A. Hendricks 1885; Adlai E. Stevenson 1893–1897.

23. Benjamin Harrison: *Republican* 1889–1893. *Vice-president*: Levi P. Morton.

25. William McKinley: *Republican* 1897–1901. *Vice-presidents*: Garret A. Hobart 1897–1899; Theodore Roosevelt 1901.

26. Theodore Roosevelt: *Republican* 1901–1909. *Vice-president*: None, as Roosevelt succeeded McKinley after his death; Charles W. Fairbanks 1905–1909.

27. William Howard Taft: *Republican* 1909–1913. *Vice-president*: James S. Sherman 1909–1912.

28. Woodrow Wilson: *Democrat* 1913–1921. *Vice-president*: Thomas R. Marshall.

29. Warren G. Harding: *Republican* 1921–1923. *Vice-president*: Calvin Coolidge.

30. Calvin Coolidge: *Republican* 1923–1929. *Vice-president*: None, as Coolidge succeeded Harding after his death; Charles G. Dawes 1925–1929.

31. Herbert Hoover: *Republican* 1929–1933. *Vice-president*: Charles Curtis.

32. Franklin D. Roosevelt: *Democrat* 1933–1945. *Vice-presidents*: John N. Garner 1933–1941; Henry A. Wallace 1941–1945; Harry S. Truman 1945.

33. Harry S. Truman: *Democrat* 1945–1953. *Vice-president*: None, as Truman succeeded Roosevelt after his death; Alben W. Barkley 1949–1953.

34. Dwight D. Eisenhower: *Republican* 1953–1961. *Vice-president*: Richard M. Nixon.

35. John F. Kennedy: *Democrat* 1961–1963. *Vice-president*: Lyndon B. Johnson.

36. Lyndon B. Johnson: *Democrat* 1963–1969. *Vice-president*: None, as Johnson succeeded Kennedy after his death; Hubert H. Humphrey 1965–1969.

37. Richard M. Nixon *Republican* 1969–1974. *Vice-presidents*: Spiro T. Agnew 1969–1973; Gerald R. Ford 1973–1974.

38. Gerald R. Ford: *Republican* 1974–1977. *Vice-president*: Nelson A. Rockefeller.

39. Jimmy Carter: *Democrat* 1977–1981. *Vice-president*: Walter F. Mondale

40. Ronald Reagan: *Republican* 1981–1989. *Vice-president*: George Bush.

41. George Bush: *Republican* 1989–1993. *Vice-president*: Dan Quayle

42. Bill Clinton: *Democrat* 1993–. *Vice-president*: Albert Gore, Jr.

Famous Quotes
from the Presidents

"No man is above the law and no man below it." — **Theodore Roosevelt**.

"Interest does not tie nations together, it sometimes separates them. But sympathy and understanding do unite them." — **Woodrow Wilson**.

"'Tis better to be alone than in bad company." — **George Washington**.

"Eternal vigilance is the price of liberty." — **Thomas Jefferson**.

"All men are equally entitled to the full and free exercise of their religion." — **James Madison**.

"Farming looks mighty easy when your plow is a pencil and you're a thousand miles from the corn field." — **Dwight D. Eisenhower**.

"Ask not what your country can do for you; ask what you can do for your country." — **John F. Kennedy**.

"The truth is found when men are free to pursue it."
"The nation that destroys its soul destroys itself." — **Franklin D. Roosevelt**.

"As I would not be a slave, so I would not be a master. This expresses my idea of democracy. Whatever differs from this, to the extent of the difference, is no democracy." — **Abraham Lincoln**.

"If you can't stand the heat, get out of the kitchen." — **Harry S. Truman**.

"Many Americans live on the outskirts of hope, some because of their poverty and some because of their color, and all too many because of both. Our task is to help reduce their despair with opportunity." — **Lyndon B. Johnson**.

Fun Facts
About the Presidents

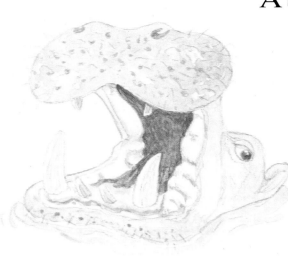

George Washington's favorite set of false teeth were made from hippopotamus teeth.

At 5'4", James Madison was the shortest president.

A tailor before he became president, Andrew Johnson made his own clothes while in office.

George Bush was the youngest commissioned naval pilot in World War II, in 1942, when he was 18 years old.

At 6'2" tall and over 300 pounds, William Taft was so large he sometimes got stuck in the White House bathtub; he ordered a new one, large enough to hold four workmen.

Ulysses S. Grant once received a speeding ticket in Washington, D.C., while driving his team of horses.

Theodore Roosevelt had animal heads from his hunting expeditions mounted in the State Dining Room.

Two strong political foes, John Adams and Thomas Jefferson, died on the same day.

A true food-lover, Thomas Jefferson brought foreign foods to America, including waffles from Holland and baked Alaska, an ice cream dessert, from France. He spent hours gardening and raised some unusual crops.

The heavy-set Grover Cleveland once admitted to a friend that he much preferred "pickled herring, Swiss cheese, and a chop" to the delicate French cuisine served at White House banquets.

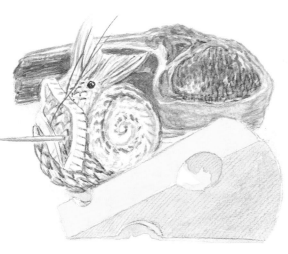

Cited for "wild dancing," Dwight D. Eisenhower was demoted from sergeant to private while attending West Point.

In 1976, President Carter's daughter, Amy, became the first presidential child to attend public school since Theodore Roosevelt's time.

Ice cream appeared at White House parties for the first time when Madison was president.

Andrew Jackson was only 13 years old when he fought in the Revolutionary War, serving as a messenger on horseback.

Until the late 19th century, the White House was kept unlocked. During Martin Van Buren's term, a vagrant came inside to spend the night on a sofa.

Harry Truman was the only president in the 20th century who did not attend college.

Believing it was more democratic, Jefferson always seated dinner guests around a circular table.

John Tyler had the most children of any U.S. president — 15 by his two wives.

Eisenhower was the first president to hold a pilot's license. He earned his during military training in the late 1930s.

A candy bar was named after Baby Ruth, daughter of the Grover Clevelands and the first baby ever born in the White House. Teddy Bears were named after President Theodore Roosevelt.

Index

A

Abolitionist movement, 22
Adams, Abigail Smith, 10
Adams, John Quincy, 5, 14, 15, 52
Adams, John, 10, 52, 54
Adams, Louisa Catherine
    Johnson, 14
Agnew, Spiro T., 47
Alamo, Battle of the, 15
Alien Act, 10
Amendments, 13th, 25; 16th, 35;
    20th, 36
American Federation of Labor
    (AFL), 31
American Relief Administration, 39
Antietam, Battle of, 25
Aroostook War, 16
Arthur, Chester A., 30, 52
Arthur, Ellen Lewis Herndon, 30
Atlanta campaign, 32

B

Bank of the United States, 9, 15
Berlin Wall, 50
Bill of Rights, 9, 12
Boxer Rebellion, 39
Brown, John, rebellion at
    Harper's Ferry, 23
Bryan, William Jennings, 33
Buchanan, James, 23, 52
Bush, Barbara Pierce, 50
Bush, George, 50, 52, 54

C

Calhoun, John C., 21
Capitol building, 4, 12
Carter, Jimmy, 48, 52, 55
Carter, Rosalynn Smith, 48
Central Intelligence Agency
    (CIA), 50
Chattanooga, Battle of, 27
China, People's Republic of, 47
Chinese Exclusion Act, 32
Civil rights, 42, 44
Civil War, 18, 22, 25, 26, 27, 28, 29,
    30, 31, 32
Civilian Conservation Corps, 40
Clay, Henry, 21
Clean Air Act, 50
Cleveland, Frances Folsom, 31
Cleveland, Grover, 5, 31, 52, 55
Clinton, Bill, 51, 52
Clinton, Hillary Rodham, 51
Cold War, 43
Compromise of 1850, 21, 22
Confederate States of America, 25
Constellation (ship), 10
Constitution (ship), 10
Constitution, 4, 5, 6, 7, 9, 10, 12, 36
Constitutional Congress, first and
    second, 8
Constitutional Convention, 9;
    Virginia, 13
Continental Army, 9
Coolidge, Calvin, 38, 52
Coolidge, Grace Anna Goodhue,
    38

D

D-Day invasion, 43
Davis, Jefferson, 25
Declaration of Independence, 10,
    11, 12

Douglas, Stephen, 22, 25
Dred Scott, 23

E

Eisenhower, Dwight David, 43,
    46, 52, 53, 55
Eisenhower, Mamie Geneva
    Doud, 43
Election process, 4
Electoral college, 4, 5; votes, 28
Emancipation Proclamation, 25
Equal Rights Amendment, 47

F

Fair Employment Practices Act, 42
Fair Housing Act, 50
Federal Farm Board, 39
Federal Hall, 9
Federal Trade Commission, 36
Federalist party, 10
Fillmore, Abigail Powers, 21
Fillmore, Millard, 21, 52
Ford, Elizabeth Bloomer, 47
Ford, Gerald R., 46, 47, 52
Fourteen Points program, 36
French-Indian Wars, 8

G

Gag rule, 14
Gardiner, Julia, 18
Garfield, James A., 29, 30, 52
Garfield, Lucretia Rudolph, 29
Gettysburg Address, 25
Gold rush, 20
Gold standard, 33
Government, branches of, 6;
    checks and balances, 6
Grain embargo, 48
Grant, Julia Dent, 27
Grant, Ulysses S., 27, 52, 54
Great Depression, 40, 45
Great Society program, 45

H

Harding, Florence Kling
    De Wolfe, 37
Harding, Warren G., 37, 38, 52
Harrison, Anna Tuthill Symmes, 17
Harrison, Benjamin, 5, 31, 32, 35, 52
Harrison, Caroline Lavinia Scott, 32
Harrison, William H., 17, 52
Hayes, Lucy Ware Webb, 28
Hayes, Rutherford B., 5, 7, 28, 52
Health Care Task Force, 51
Health, Education, and Welfare,
    Department of, 43
Hiroshima, 42
Hoover Commission, 39
Hoover Dam, 39
Hoover, Herbert, 39, 52
Hoover, Lou Henry, 39
Hostage crisis, 48

I

Immigrants, European, 31
Impeach, right to, 7
Inauguration, 5
Income tax, 35
Irangate, 49

J

Jackson, Andrew, 12, 14, 15, 16,
    19, 52, 55
Jackson, Rachel Donelson, 15
Jacksonian party, 19
Jefferson, Martha Wayles
    Skelton, 11
Jefferson, Thomas, 10, 11, 12, 13,
    52, 53, 54, 55
Johnson, Andrew, 26, 52, 54

Johnson, Claudia Alta Taylor, 45
Johnson, Eliza McCardle, 26
Johnson, Lyndon B., 7, 45, 52, 53

K

Kansas-Nebraska bill, 22
Kellogg-Briand Pact, 38
Kennedy, John F., 44, 45, 51, 52, 53
King, Jr., Martin Luther, 45
Korean War, 42
Ku Klux Klan, 27

L

Land rush, Oklahoma, 32
Lane, Harriet, 23
League of Nations, 36
Lee, General Robert E., 25, 27
Lincoln, Abraham; campaign, 5, 24;
    Memorial, 25; presidency, 5,
    26, 29, 52; quotes, 53
Lincoln, Mary Todd, 24
Louisiana Purchase, 11, 13
Lusitania, sinking of the, 36

M

MacArthur, General Douglas, 43
Madison, Dolley Payne Todd, 12
Madison, James, 9, 12, 52, 53, 54, 55
Maine (battleship), 33
Manifest Destiny, 19
Marshall, Chief Justice John, 7
McKinley, Ida Saxton, 33
McKinley, William, 33, 34, 52
Mexican War, 19, 20, 27
Middle East, 47
Missouri Compromise, 13, 23
Monroe Doctrine, 13
Monroe, Elizabeth Kortwright, 13
Monroe, James, 13, 14, 52
Monticello, 11
Mount Rushmore, 41
Mount Vernon, 8, 9

N

National convention, 4, 5
National Recovery Administration
    (NRA), 40
Native American tribes, 15, 32
New Deal, 41
New Freedom, 36
New Orleans, Battle of, 12
Nixon, Richard M., 46, 47, 52
Nixon, Thelma Catherine Ryan, 46
North American Free Trade
    Agreement (NAFTA), 51
North Atlantic Treaty Organisation
    (NATO), 43
Nuclear Test Ban Treaty, 44

O

Onassis, Jacqueline Lee Bouvier
    Kennedy, 44
Operation Desert Storm, 50

P

Pan-American Exposition, 33
Panama Canal, 34; Zone, 43
Party system, 4
Peace Conference, 1918, 36
Peace Corps, 44
Pearl Harbor, 41
Perry, Commodore Matthew, 22
Pierce, Franklin, 22, 23, 52
Pierce, Jane Means Appleton, 22
Polk, James K., 19, 23, 52
Polk, Sarah Childress, 19
Primary elections, 4

R

Red Cross, 30
Reagan, Nancy Davis, 49

Reagan, Ronald, 49, 50, 52
Republican National Committee, 50
Revolutionary War, 8, 10, 12, 13,
    55
Roosevelt, Anna Eleanor
    Roosevelt, 40
Roosevelt, Edith Kermit Carow, 34
Roosevelt, Franklin D., 7, 39, 40,
    42, 52, 53
Roosevelt, Theodore, 7, 34, 35, 52,
    53, 54, 55

S

Second Seminole War, 18
Sedition Act, 10
Sherman Anti-Trust Act, 32
Smoot-Hawley Act, 39
Social Security Act, 40; benefits, 43
Soviet Union, 47
Space race, 43, 44; astronauts, 44, 45
Spanish-American War, 33, 34
Square Deal, 34
Stamp Act, 10
Star of the West (ship), 23
State of the Union Address, 7
Statue of Liberty, 31
Supreme Court, 6, 7

T

Taft, Helen Herron, 35
Taft, William Howard, 35, 52, 53
Taylor, Margaret Mackall Smith, 20
Taylor, Zachary, 20, 21, 52
Thames, Battle of, 17
Tippecanoe, Battle of, 17
Truman, Elizabeth Virginia
    Wallace, 42
Truman, Harry S., 6, 39, 42, 52, 53,
    55
Tyler, John, 17, 18, 52, 55
Tyler, Letitia Christian, 18

U

U.S. Food Administration, 39
United Nations, 40
United States Navy, first, 10
United States (ship), 10

V

Valley Forge, Pa., 8
Van Buren, Hannah Hose, 16
Van Buren, Martin, 16, 17, 52, 55
Veto, presidential, 7, 12
Vietnam War, 45, 46, 47
Virginia Constitutional
    Convention, 13
Virginia House of Burgesses, 8

W

Wall Street crash, 39
War of 1812, 12, 17
War on Poverty, 45
Washington Monument, 31
Washington, George, 4, 6, 8, 9, 12,
    52, 53, 54, 55
Washington, Martha Dandridge
    Custis, 8
Watergate scandal, 46, 47
Webster, Daniel, 18, 21
Webster-Ashburton Treaty, 16, 18
Westward expansion, 15
White House, 6, 10, 13, 21
Wilson, Edith Bolling Galt, 36
Wilson, Woodrow, 36, 52, 53
World War I, 36, 39
World War II, 39, 41, 44, 50
Wounded Knee, Battle of, 32

Y

Yalta Conference, 41